QUICK DRAW!

How to Draw
Activity Book

ACTIVIBOOKS FOR KIDS

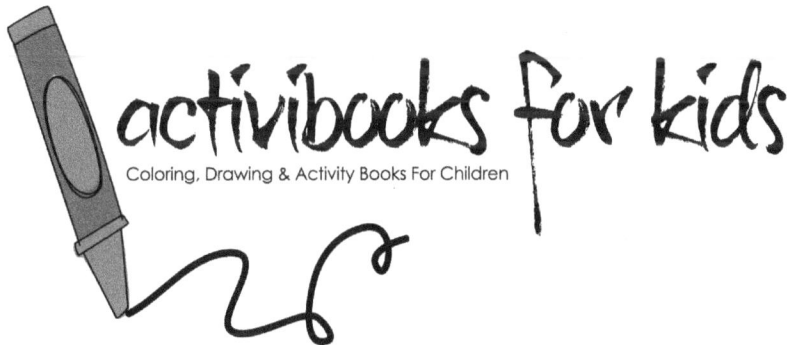

activibooks for kids
Coloring, Drawing & Activity Books For Children

All Rights reserved. No part of this book may be reproduced or used in any way or form or by any means whether electronic or mechanical, this means that you cannot record or photocopy any material ideas or tips that are provided in this book.

Copyright 2016

INSTRUCTIONS FOR DRAWING:

THIS HOW-TO DRAWING BOOK CONSISTS OF IMAGES THAT ARE PLACED ON GRIDS. THERE IS AN EMPTY DRAWING BOX WITH GRIDS THAT WILL SERVE AS YOUR PRACTICE SPACE. TO COPY EACH IMAGE, DRAW PARTS OF THE IMAGE PER GRID AND PUT THEM ON THE BLANK GRIDS. SOUNDS DIFFICULT? NOT REALLY. TRY IT FIRST!

IT'S OKAY IF YOU DON'T COPY THE IMAGE PERFECTLY. AFTER ALL, DRAWING IS ABOUT THE EXPRESSION OF YOUR PERCEPTION AS WELL AS YOUR HAND STRENGTH AND CONTROL.

WHEN YOU'VE COPIED THE IMAGE, GO AHEAD AND COLOR IT NEXT! WE'RE EXCITED TO SEE WHAT YOU CAN DO!

DRAW THE IMAGE

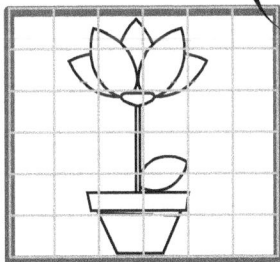

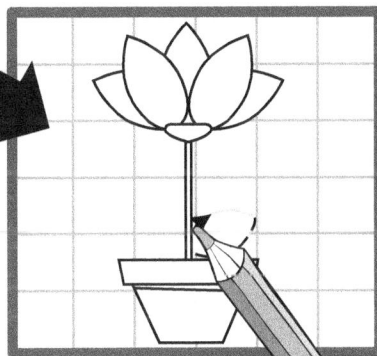

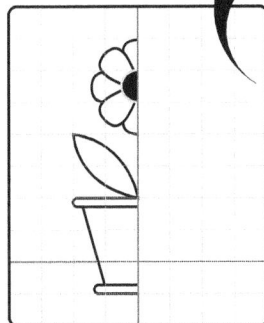

DRAW
THE
IMAGE

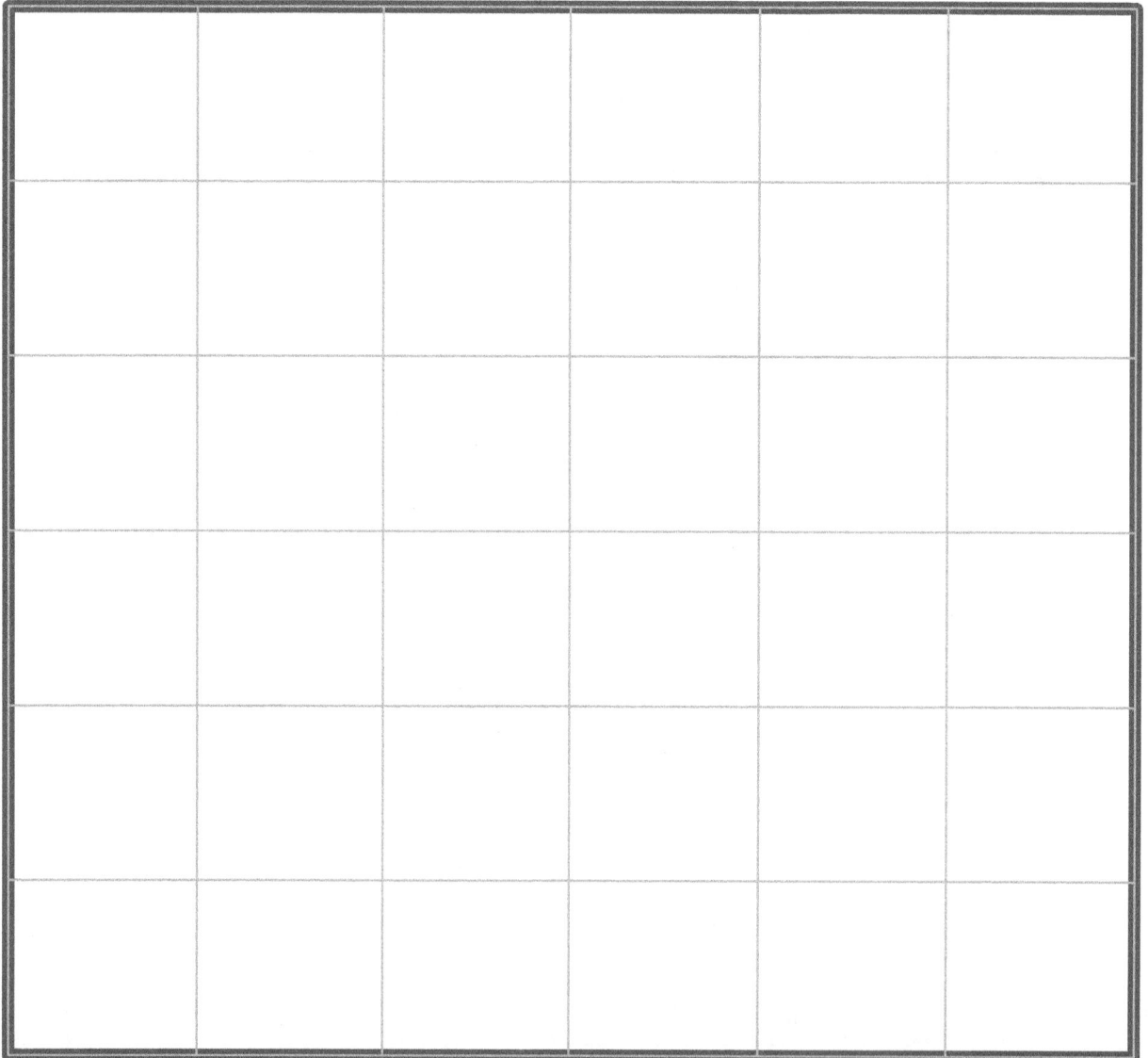

DRAW
THE
IMAGE

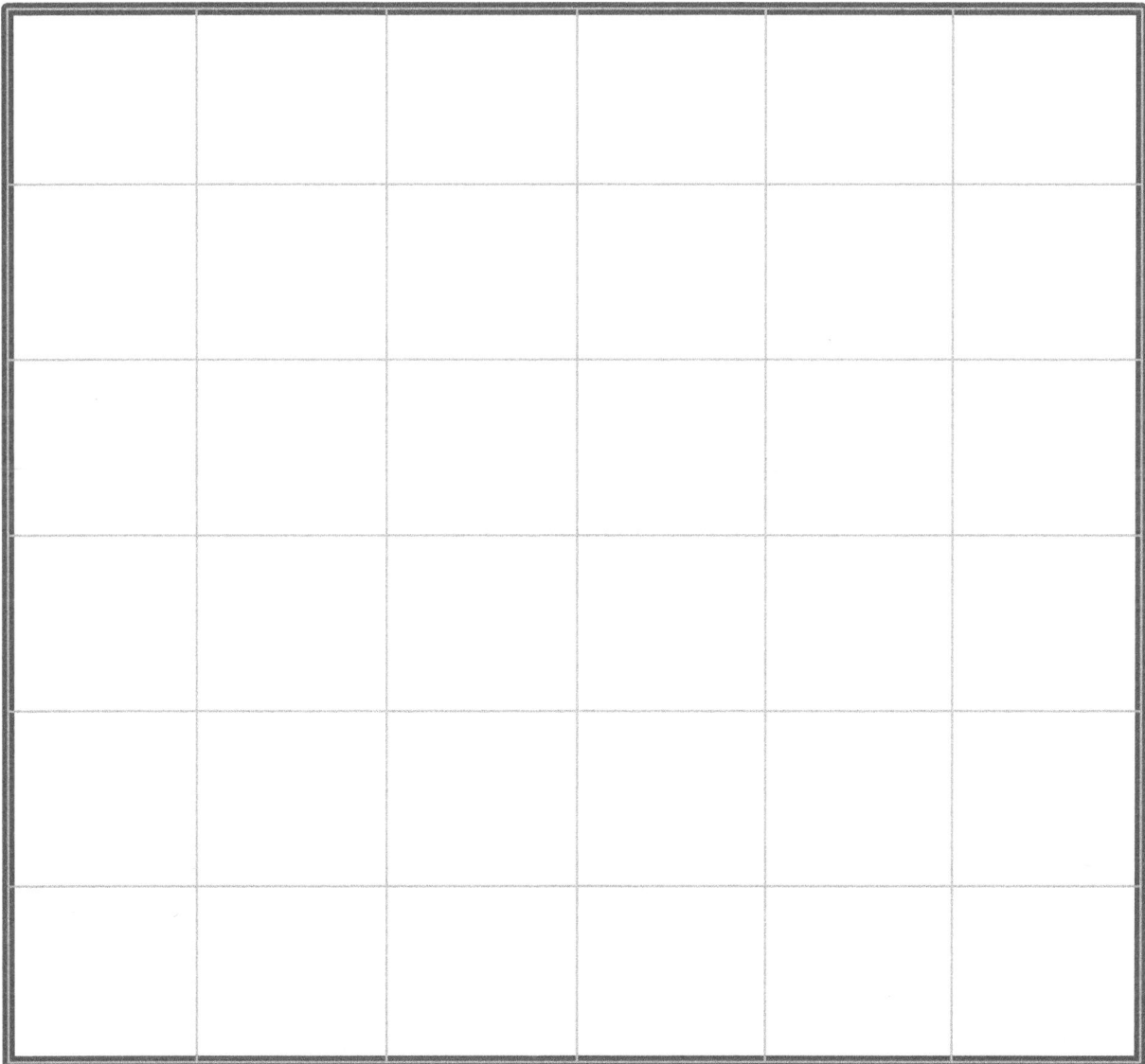

DRAW
THE
IMAGE

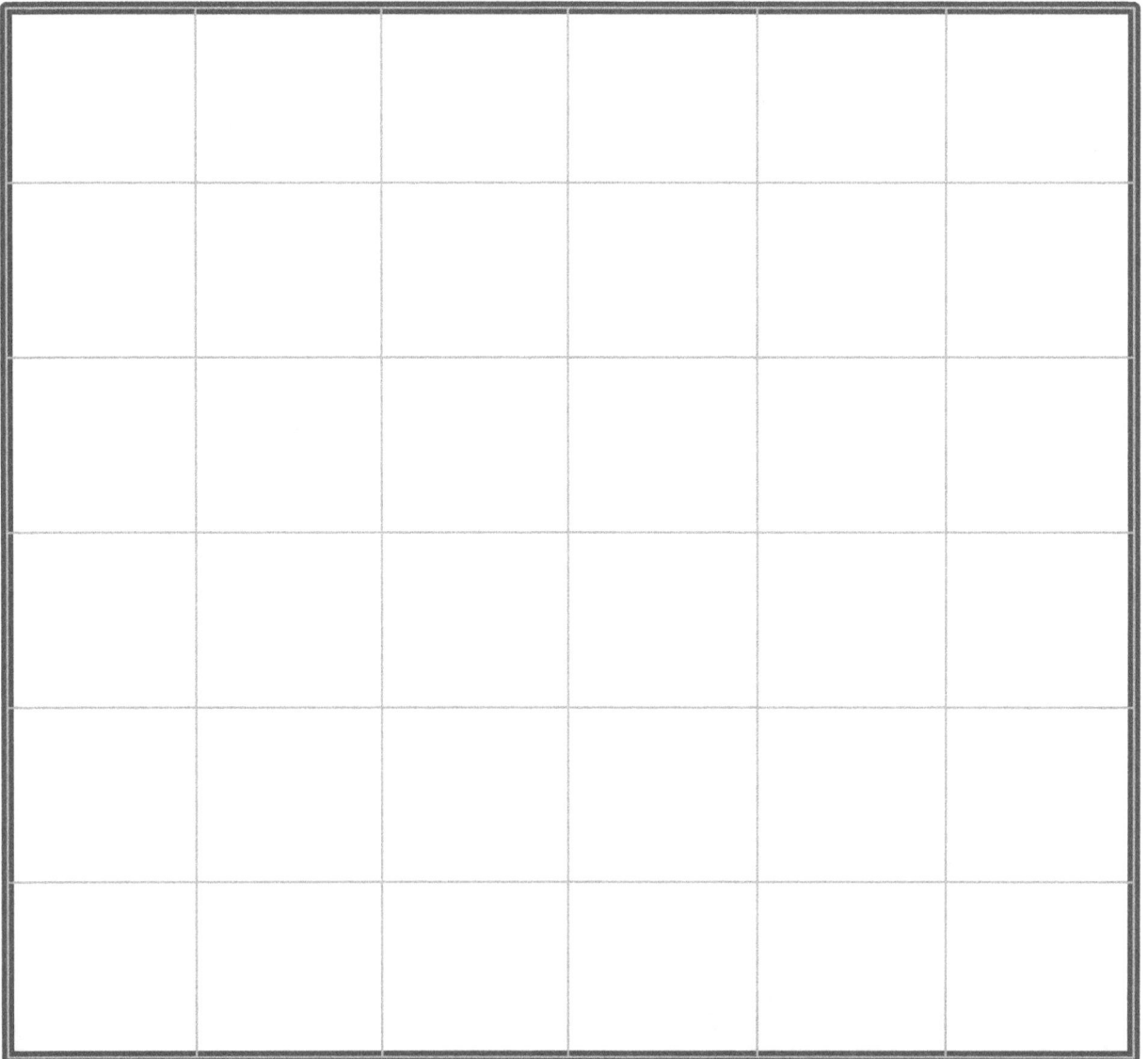

DRAW
THE
IMAGE

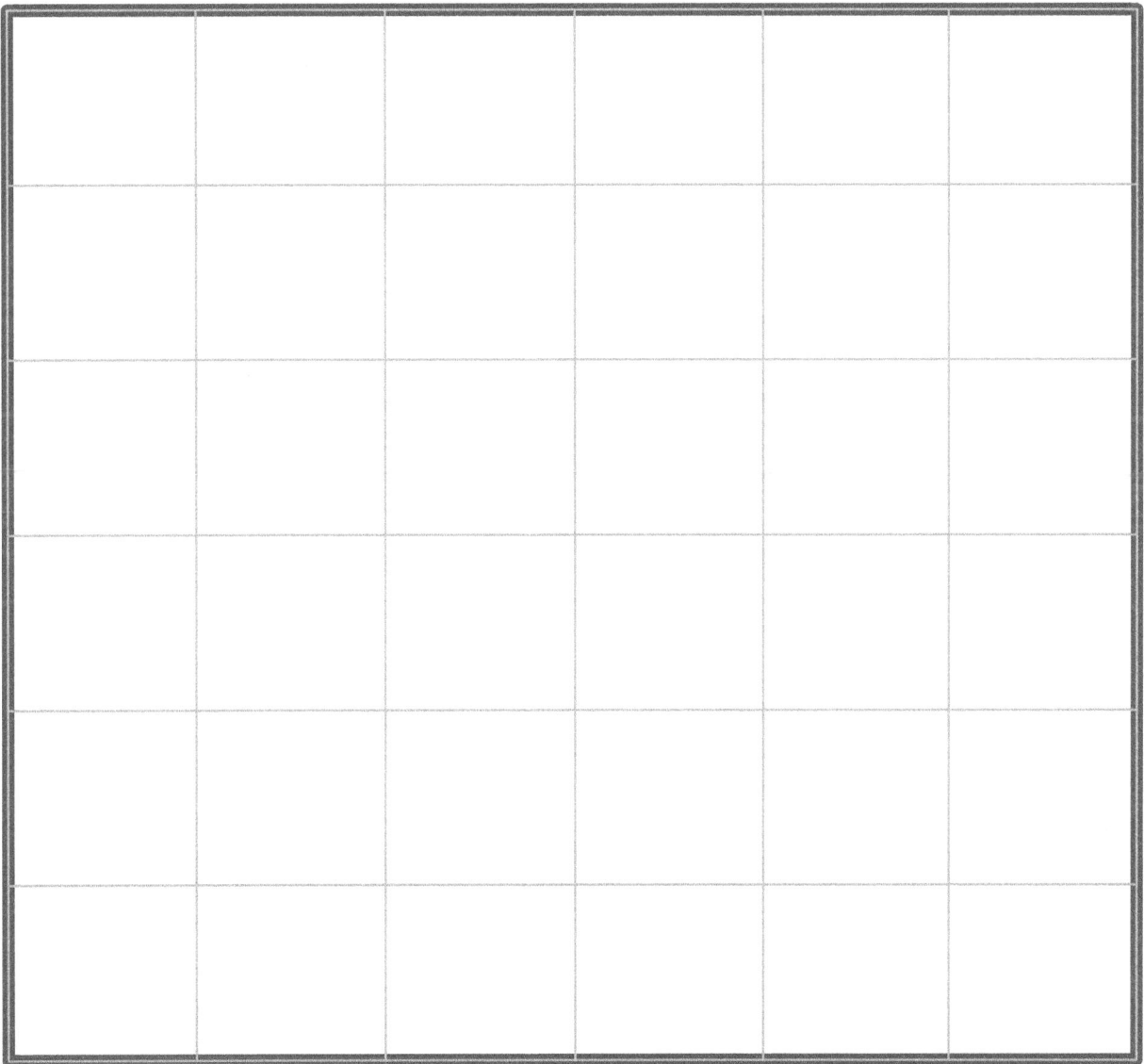

DRAW
THE
IMAGE

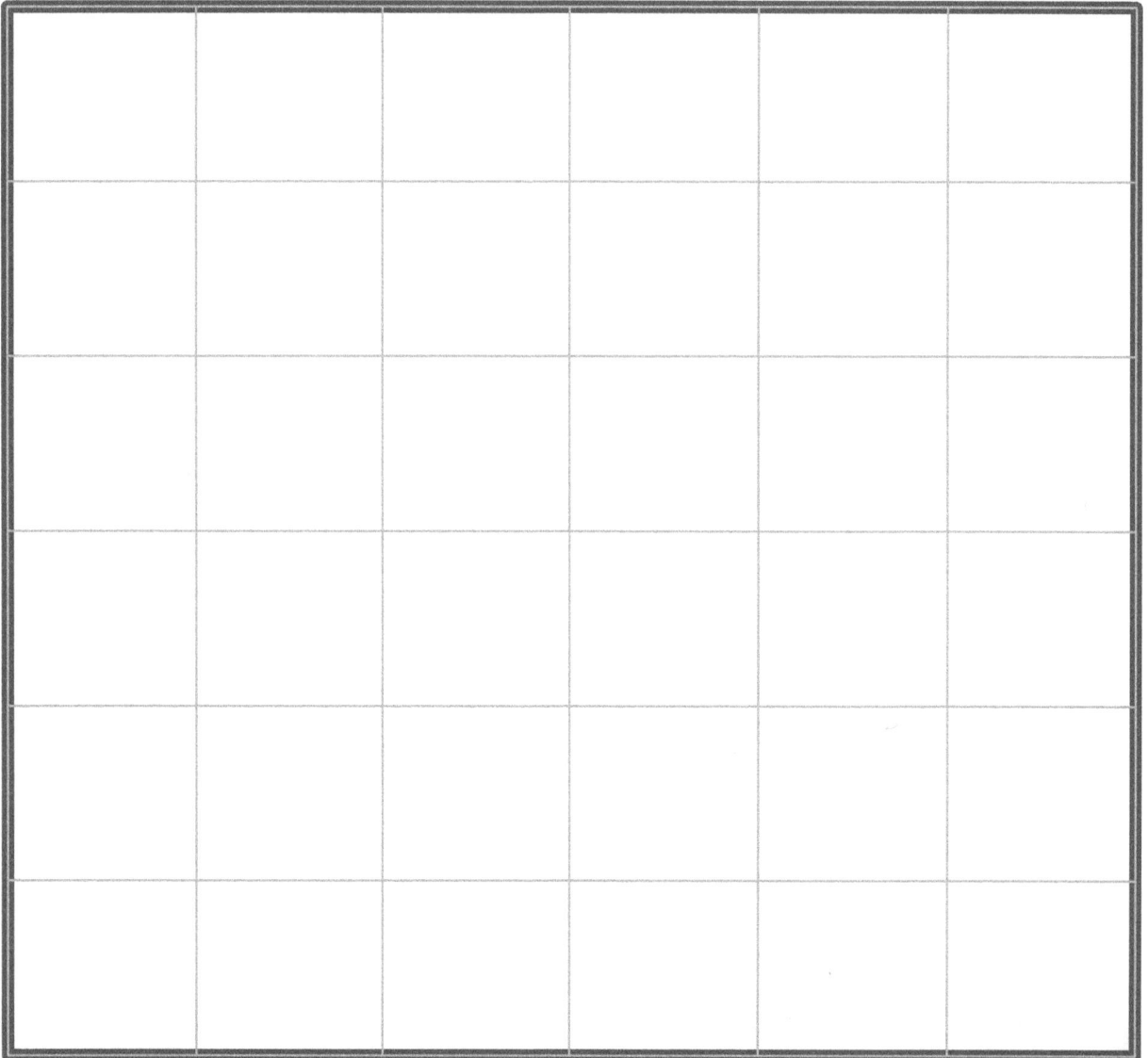

DRAW
THE
IMAGE

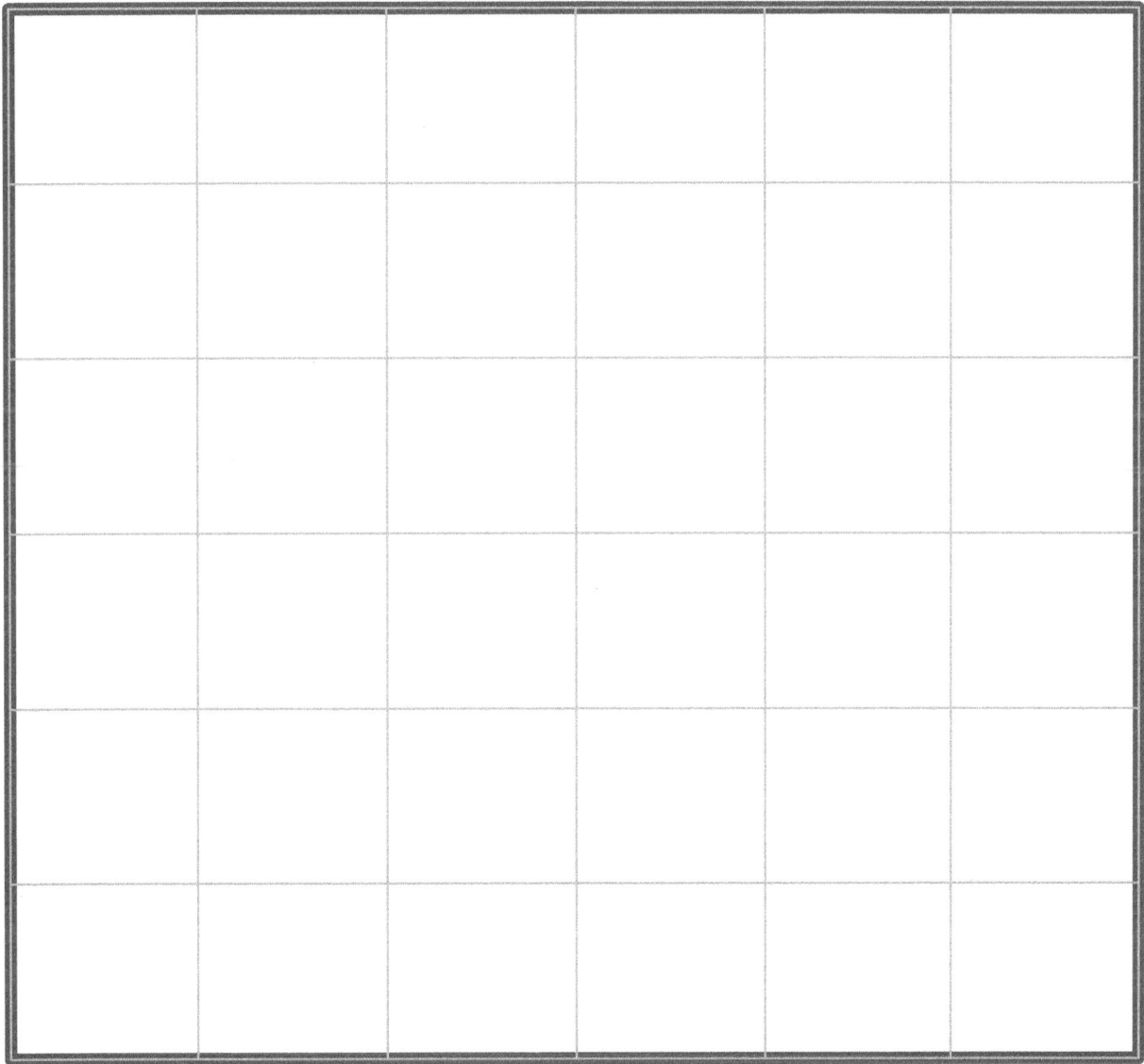

DRAW
THE
IMAGE

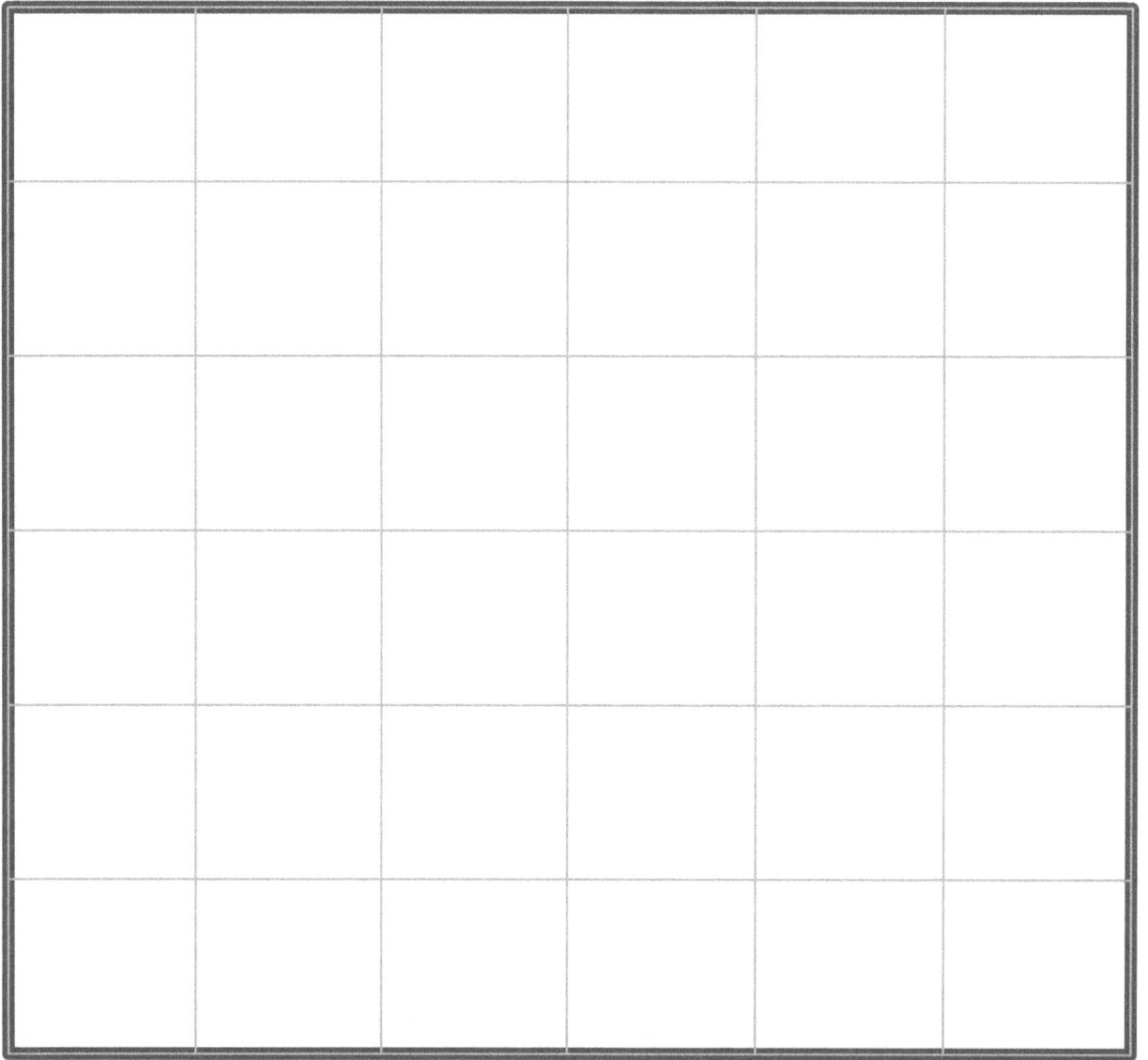

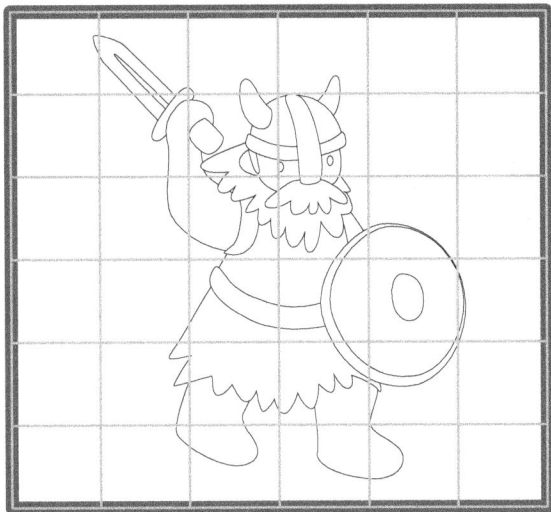

DRAW
THE
IMAGE

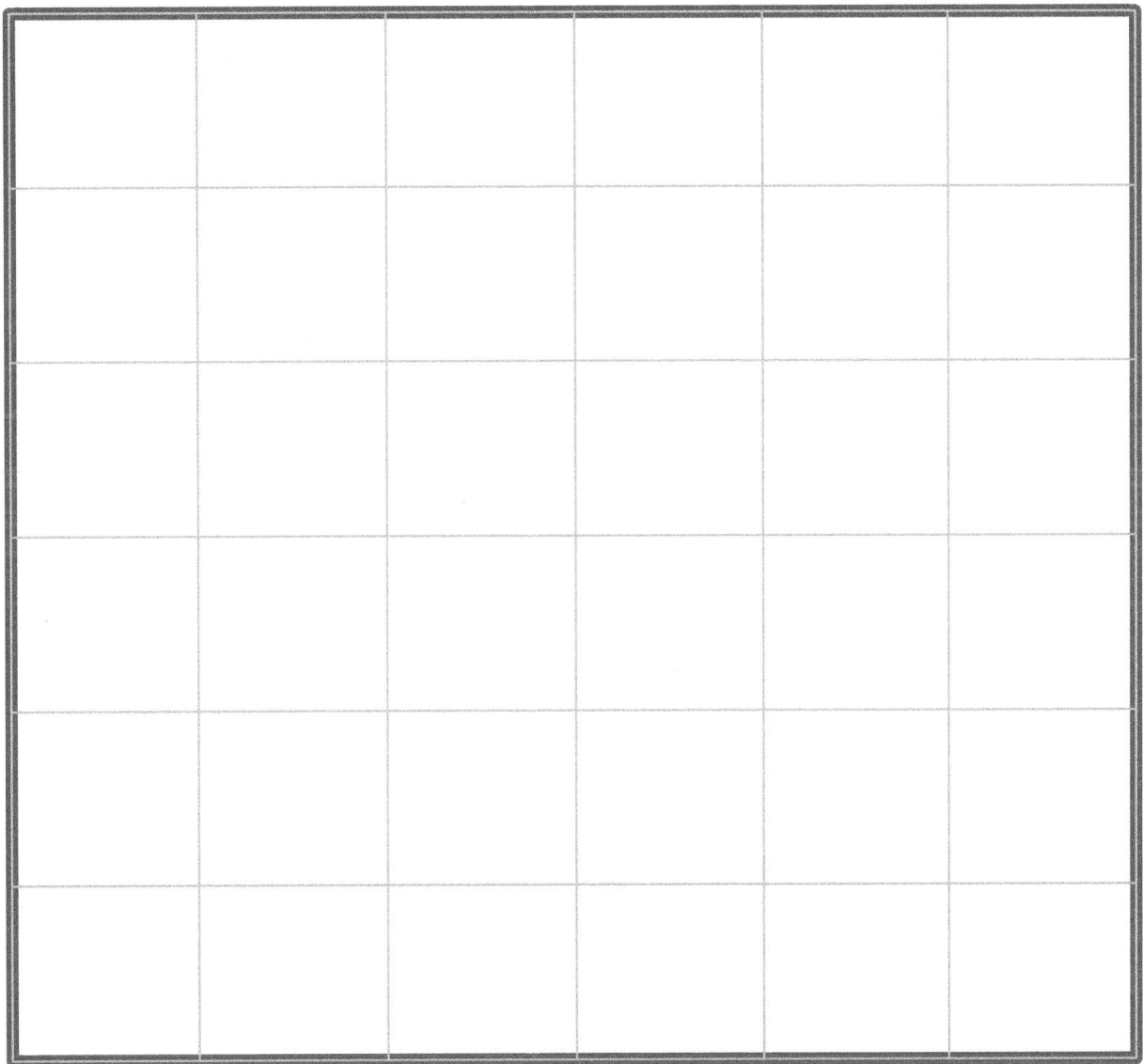

DRAW
THE
IMAGE

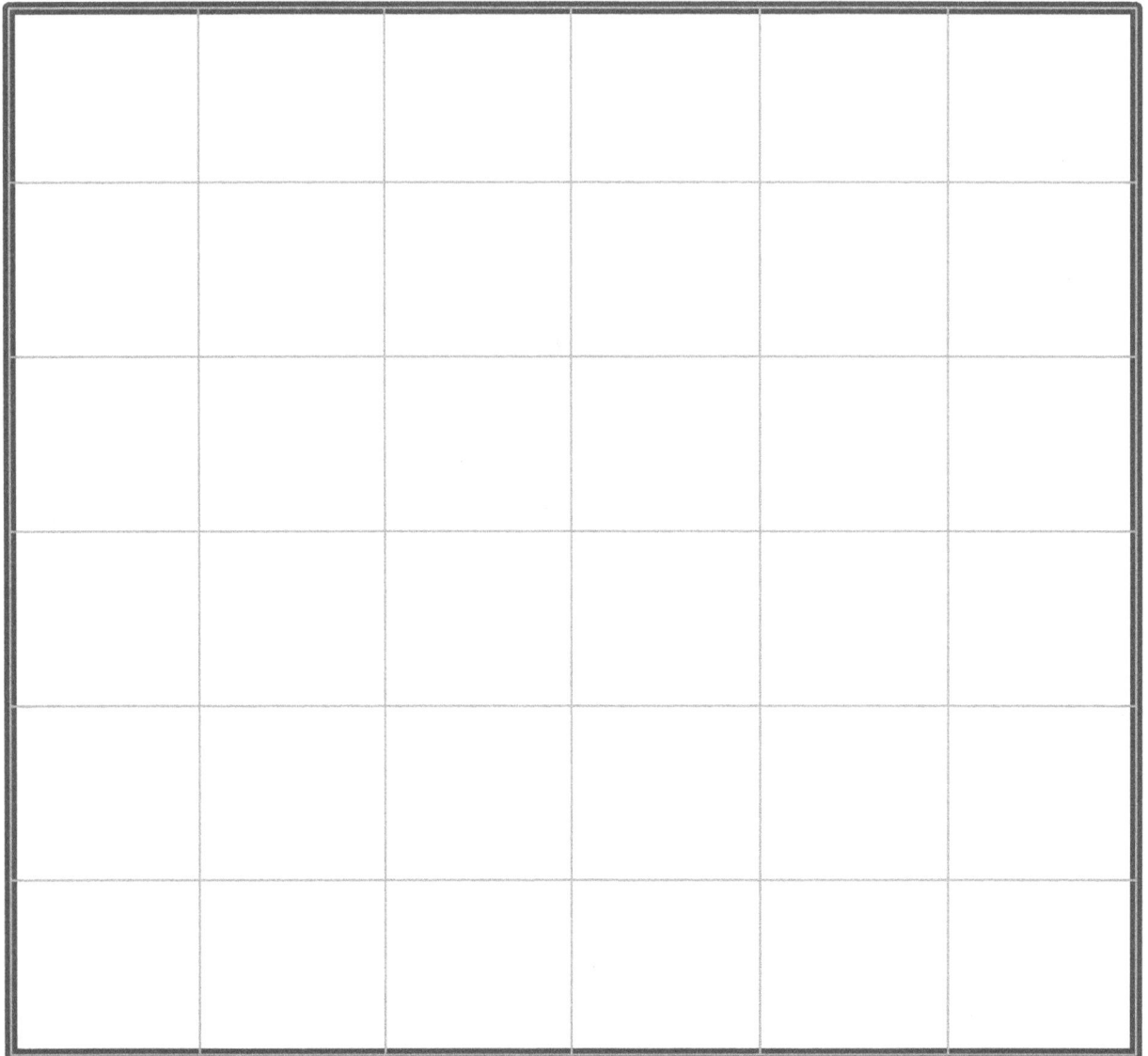

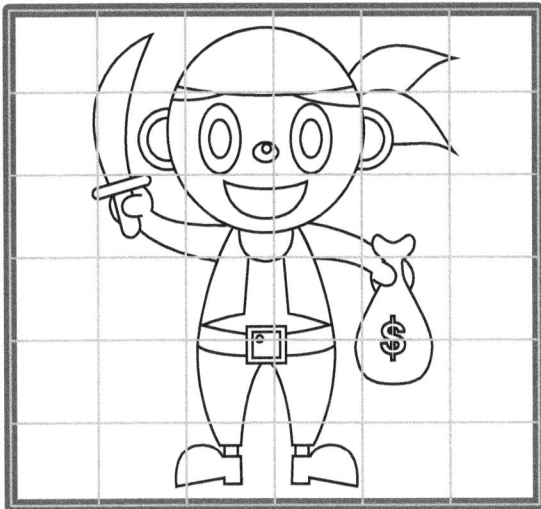

DRAW
THE
IMAGE

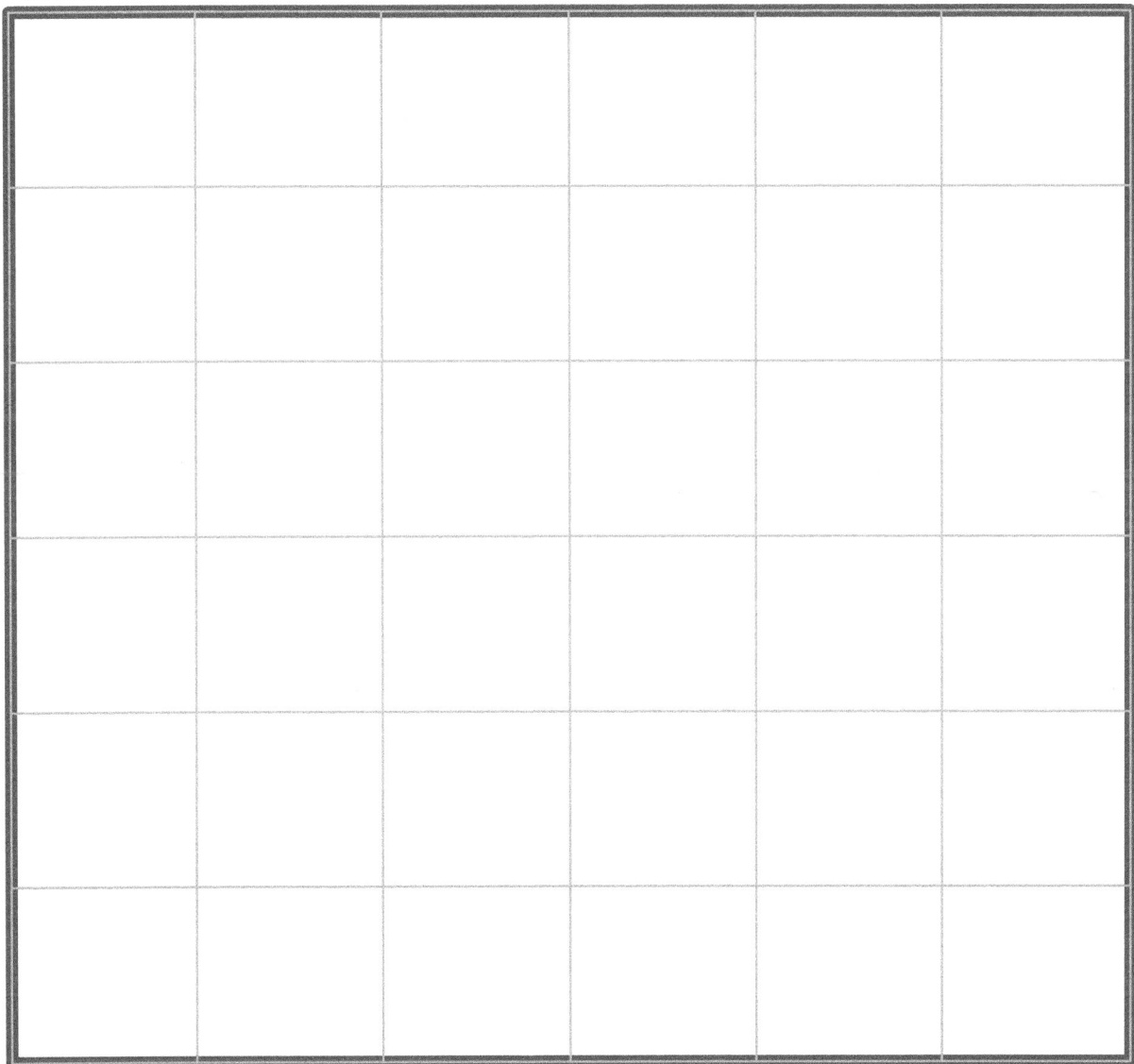

DRAW
THE
IMAGE

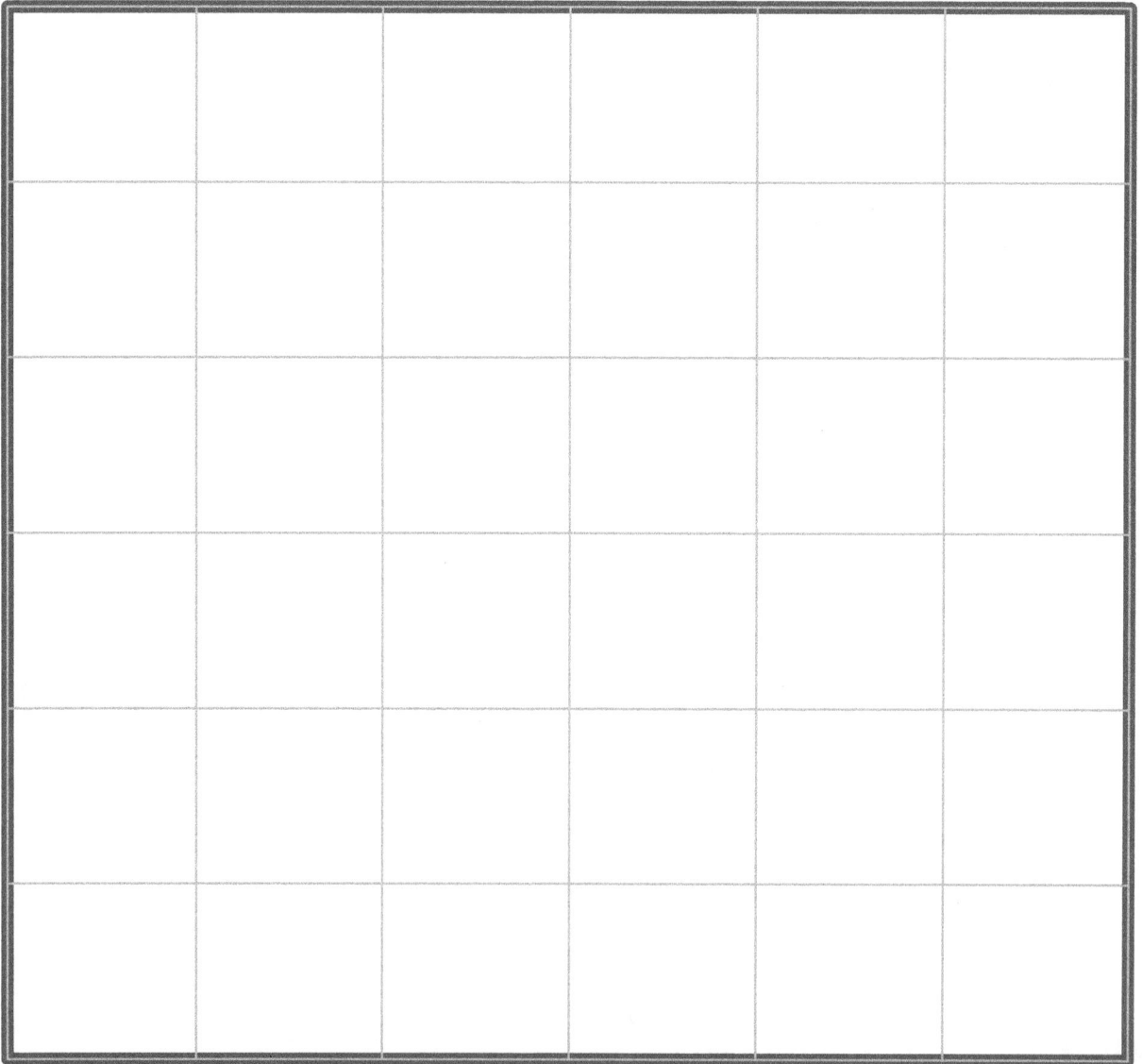

DRAW
THE
IMAGE

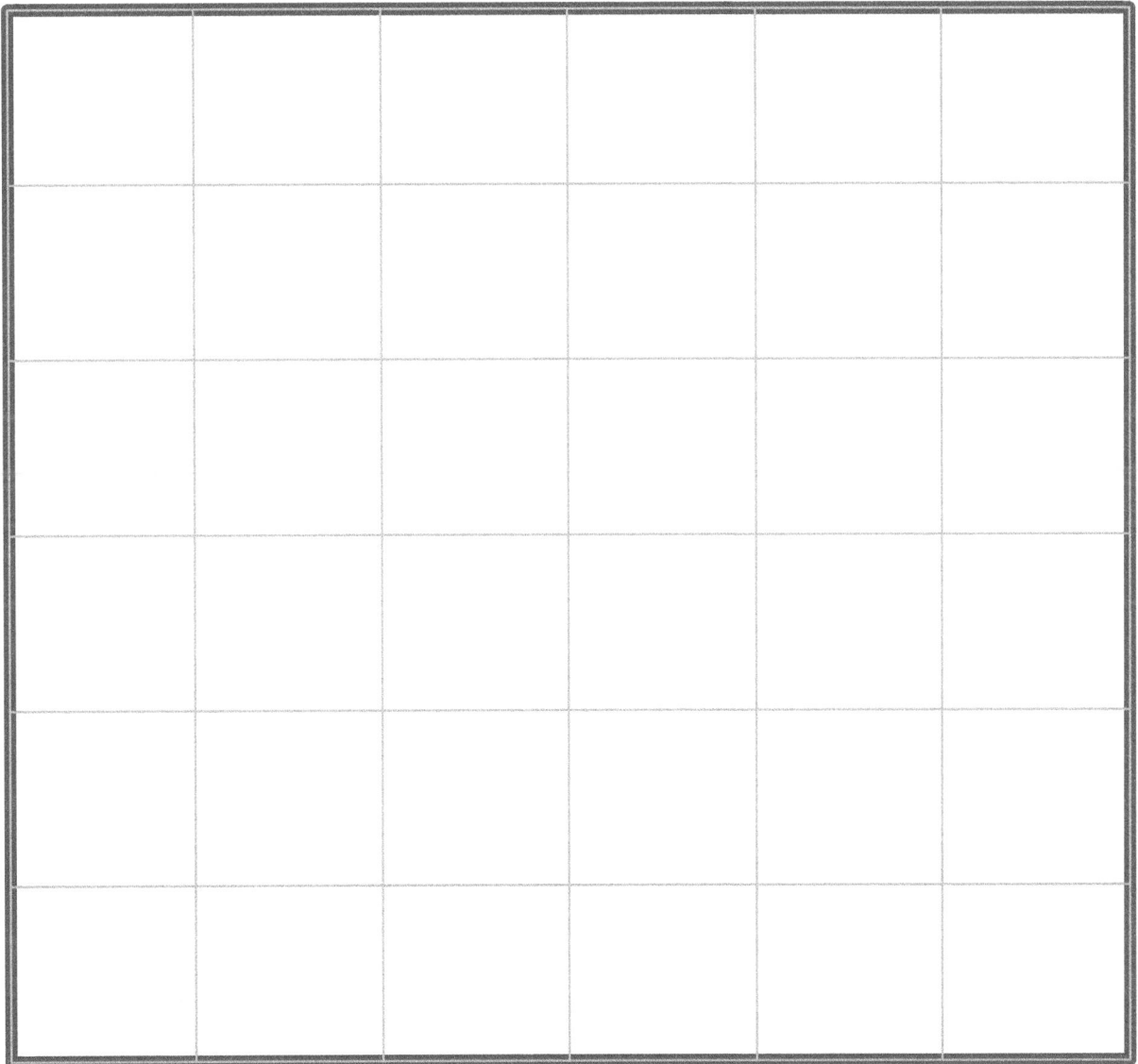

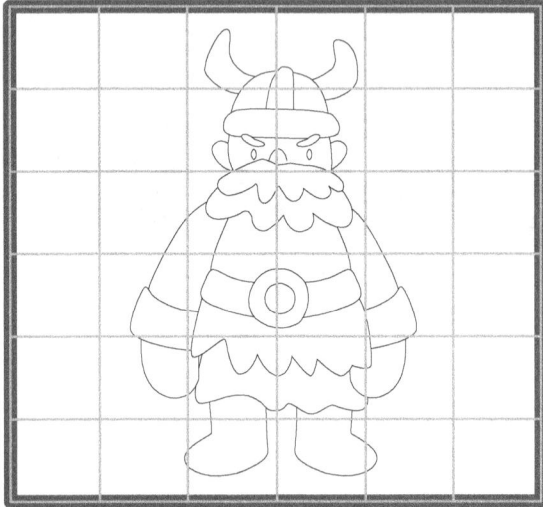

DRAW
THE
IMAGE

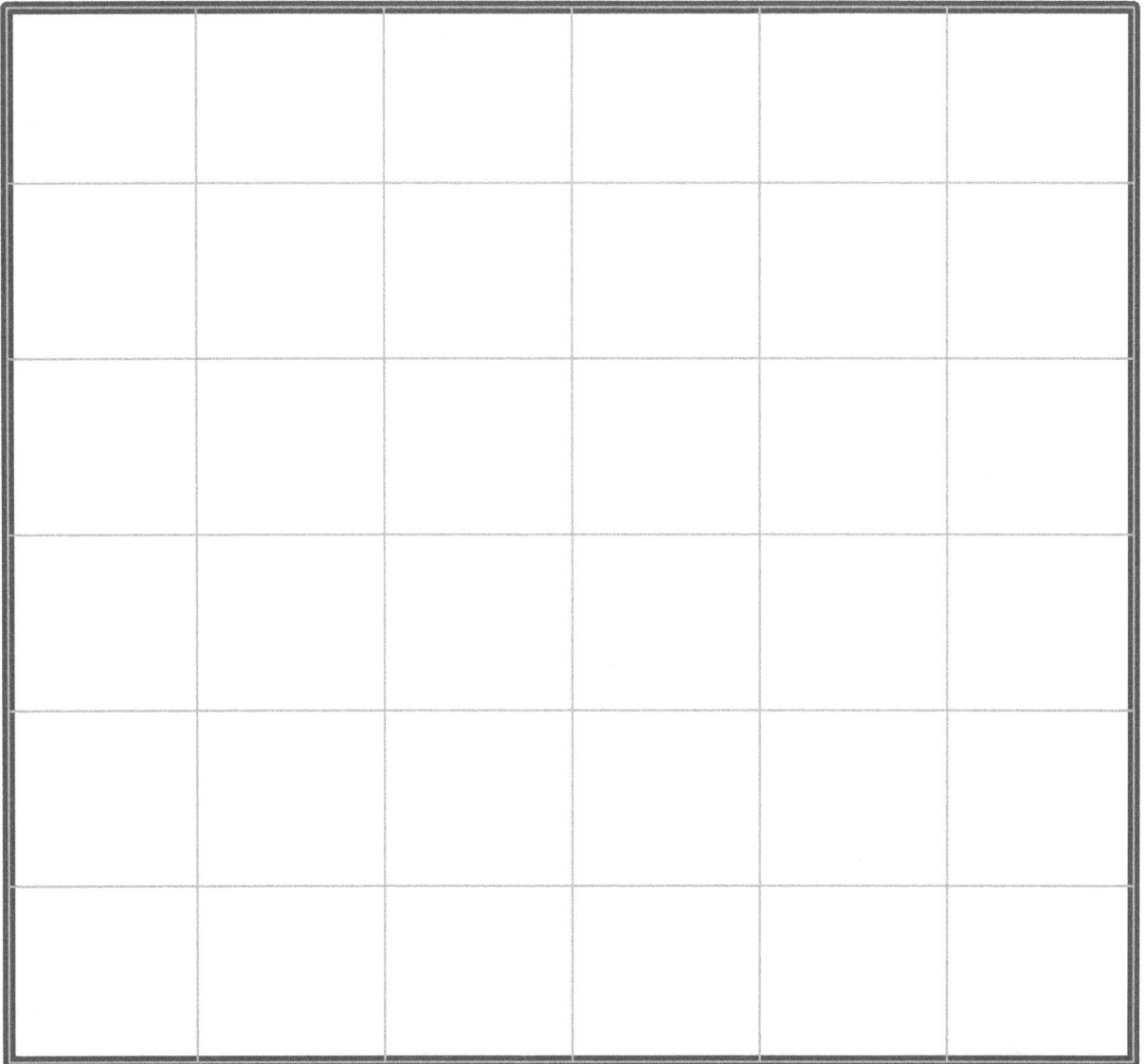

DRAW
THE
IMAGE

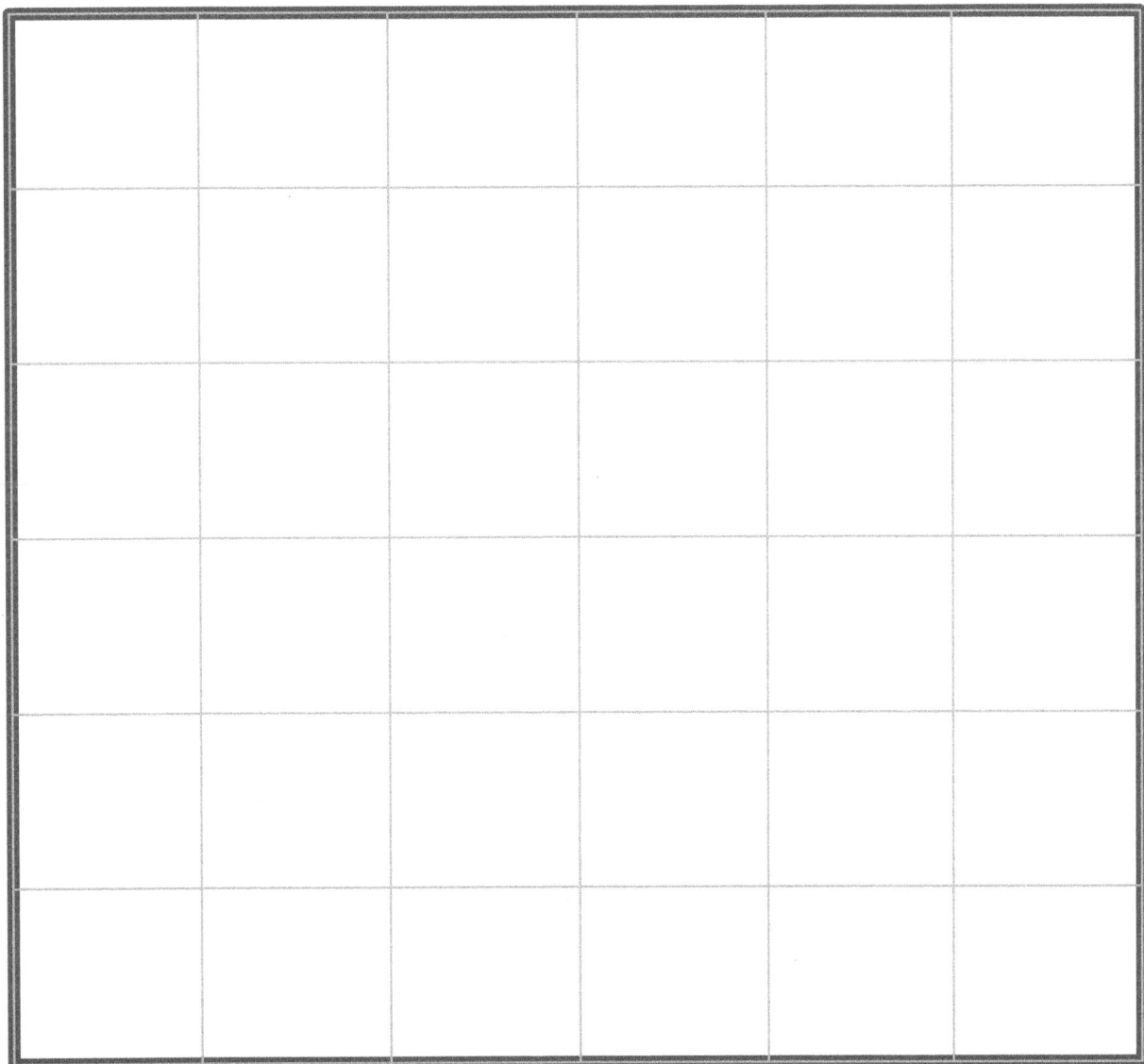

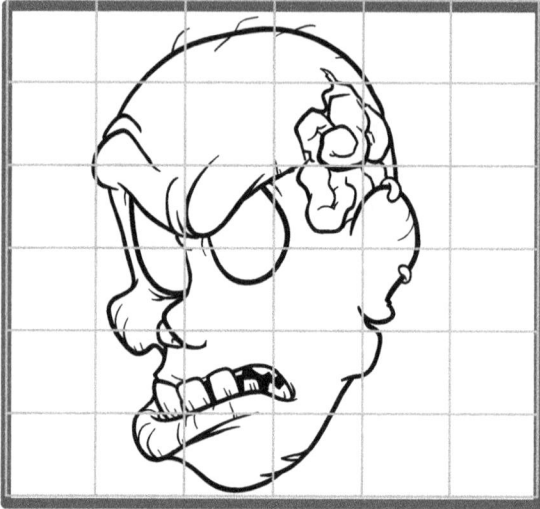

DRAW
THE
IMAGE

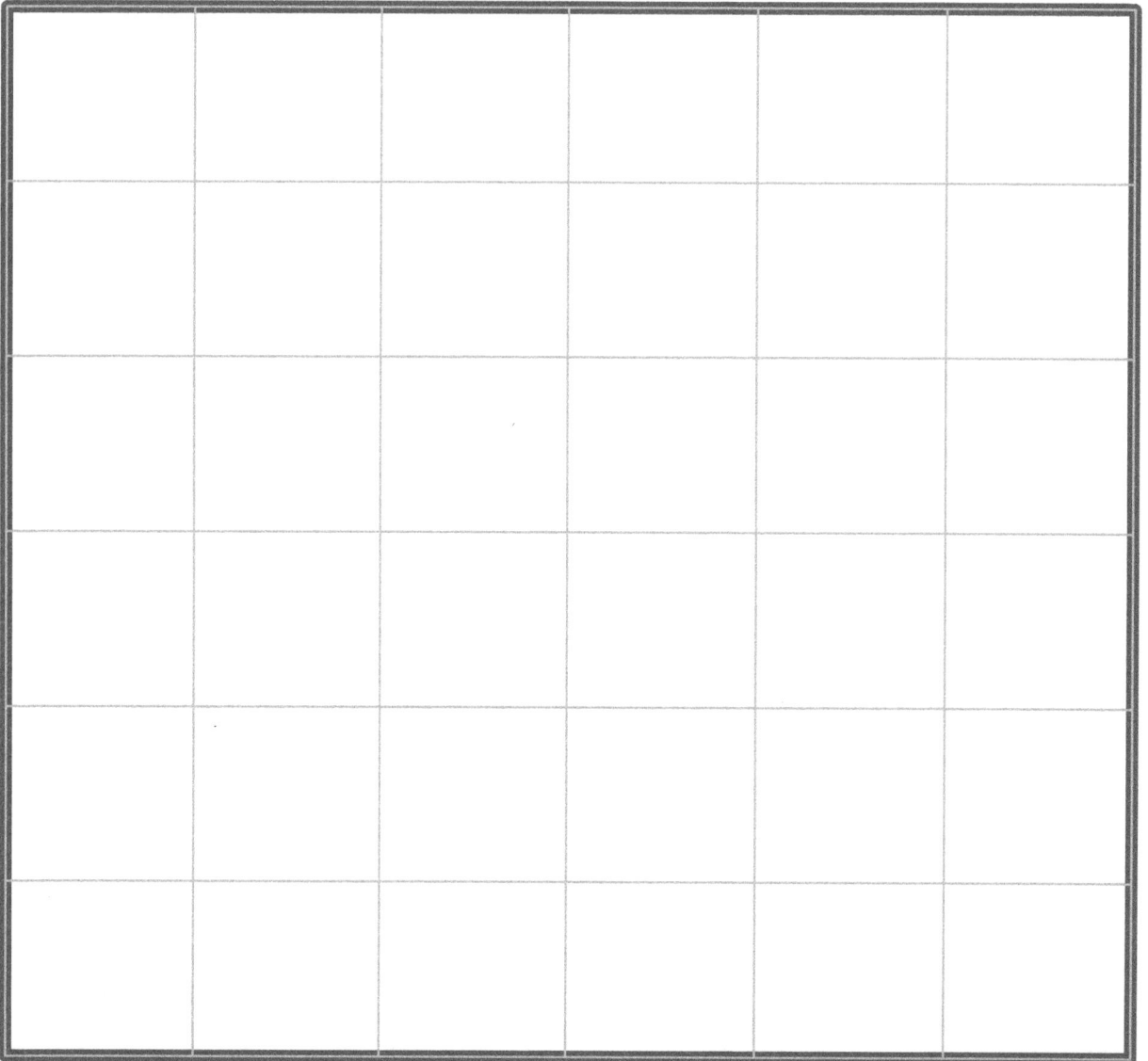

DRAW
THE
IMAGE

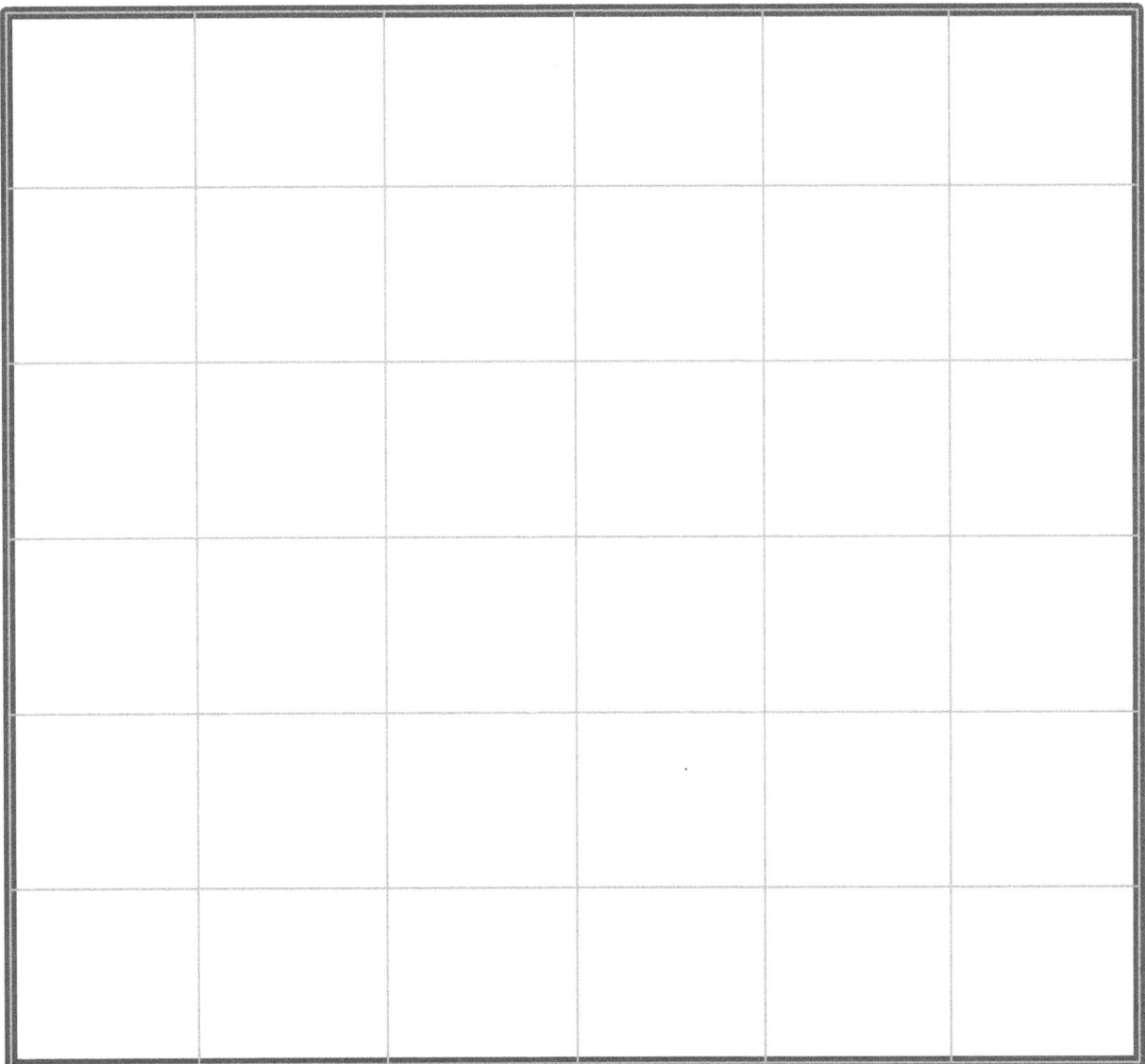

DRAW
THE
IMAGE

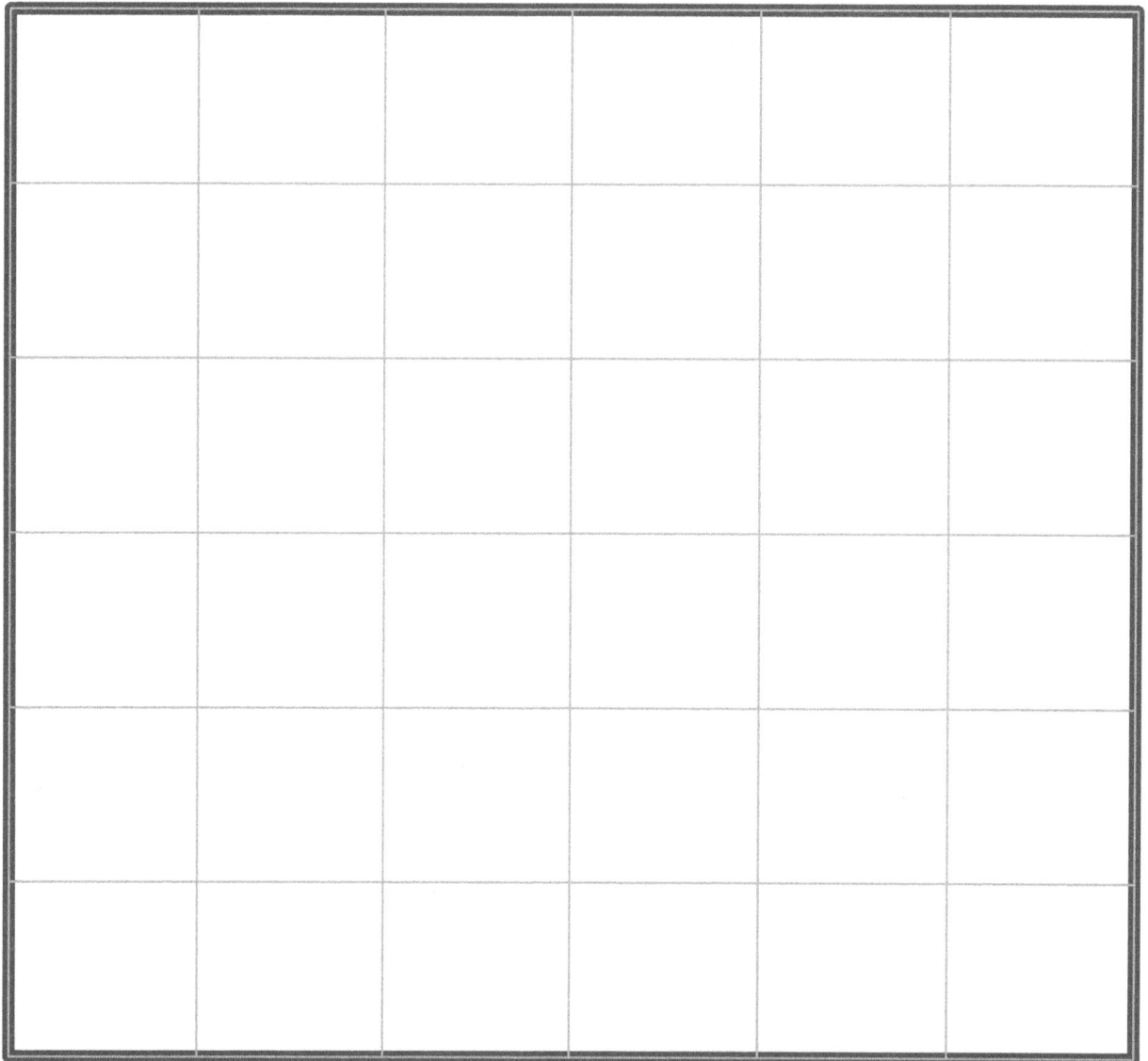

DRAW
THE
IMAGE

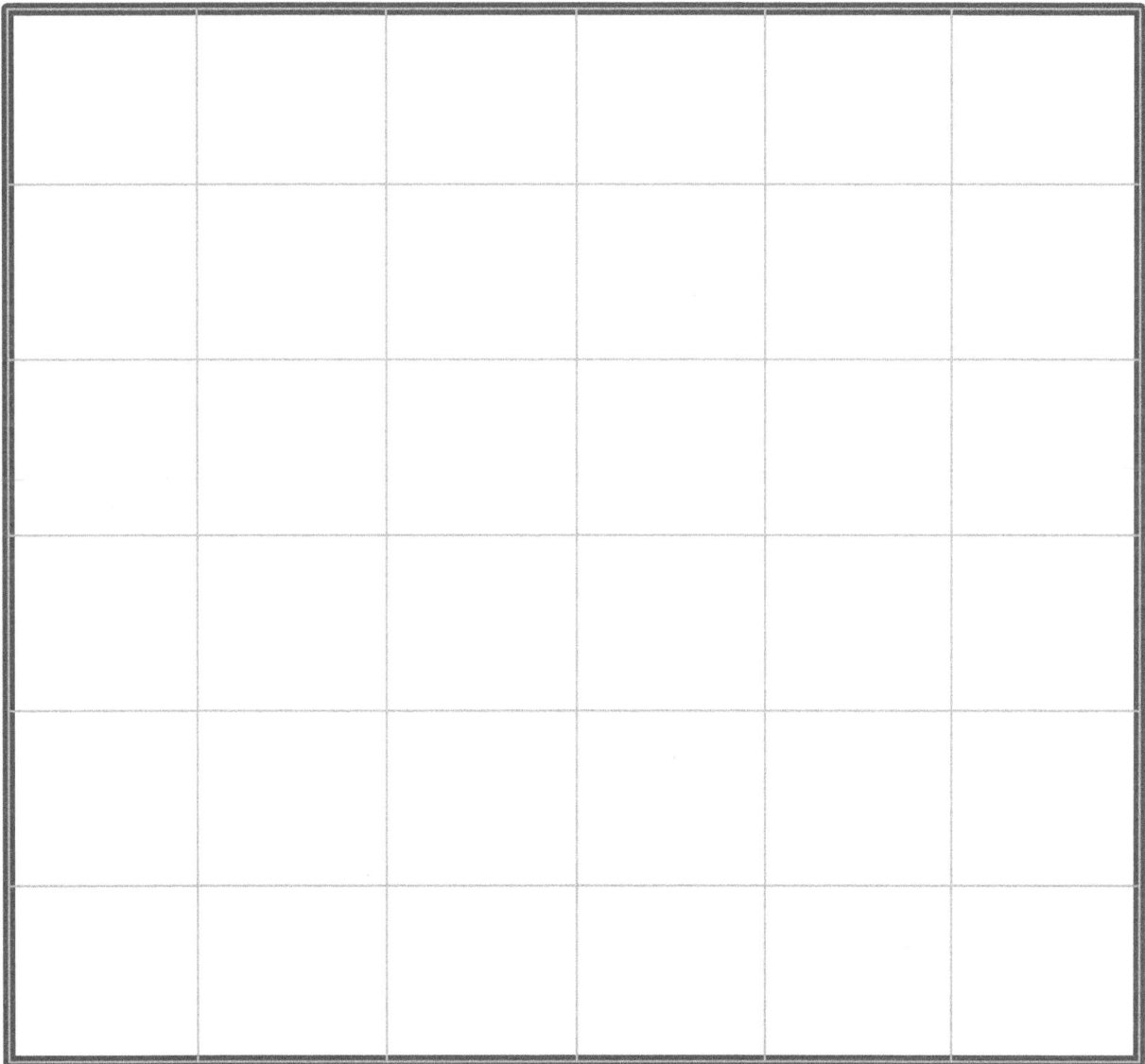

DRAW
THE
IMAGE

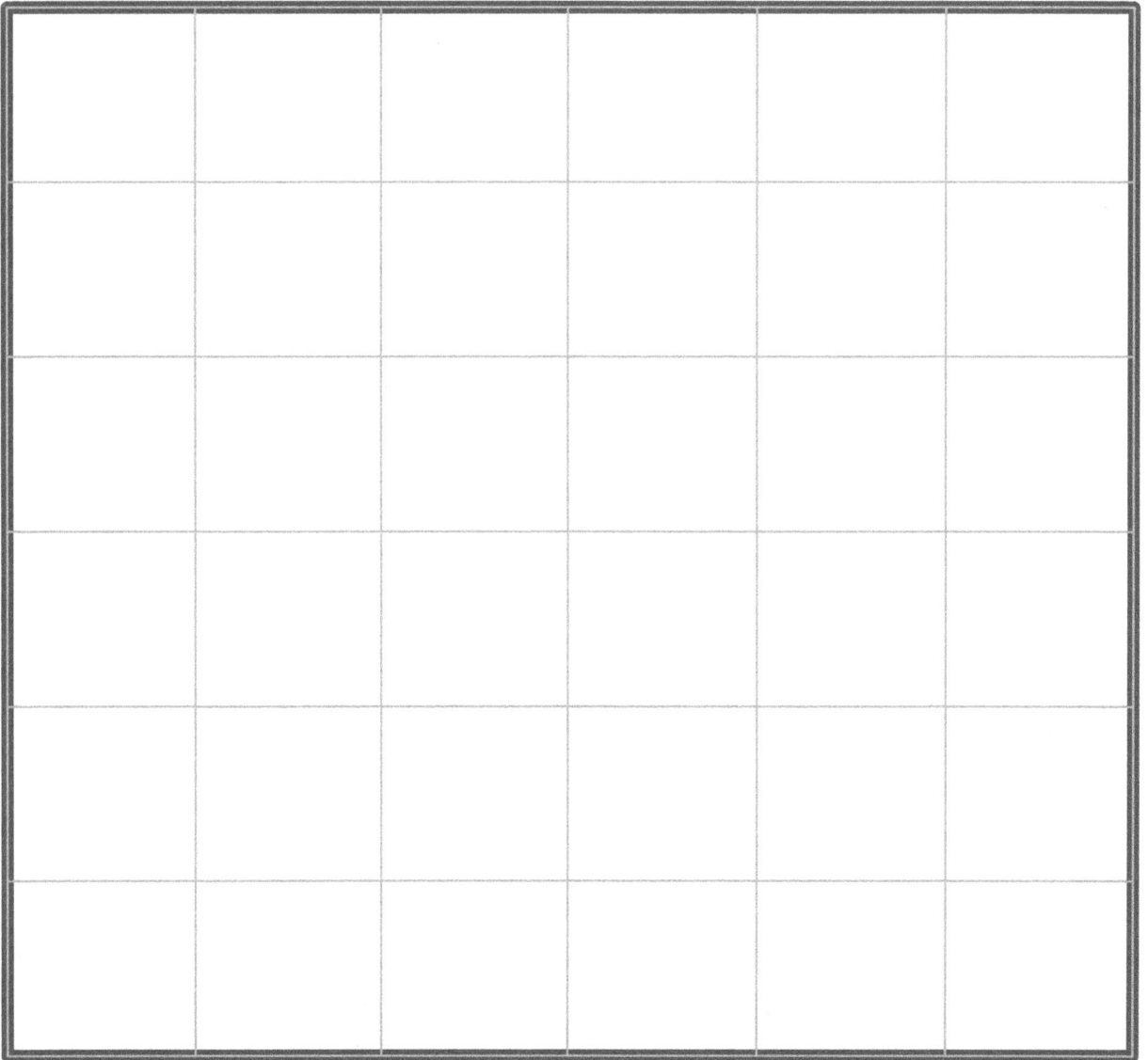

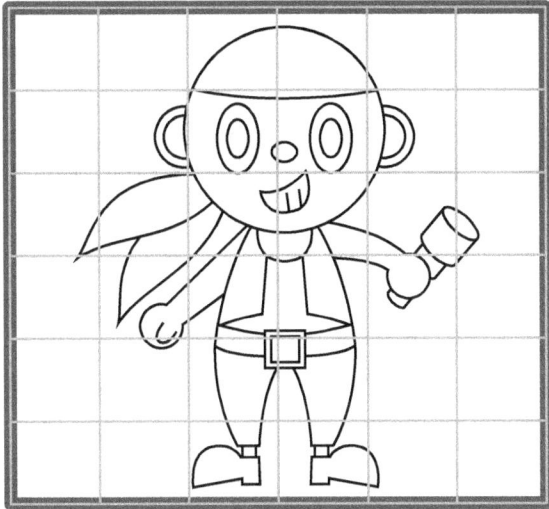

DRAW
THE
IMAGE

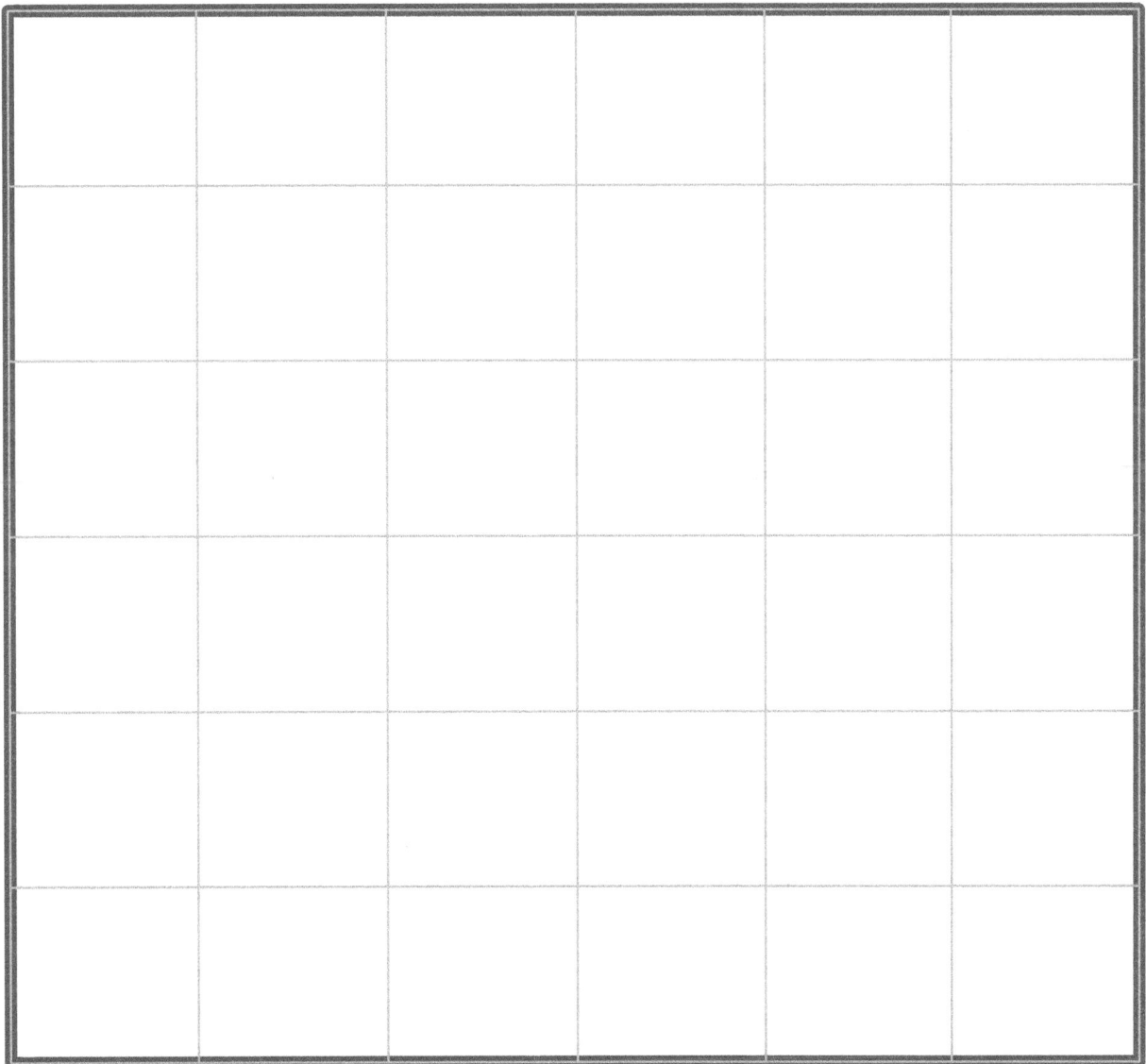

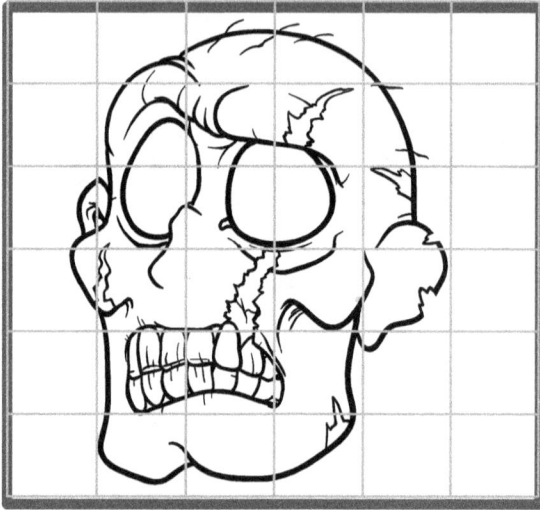

DRAW
THE
IMAGE

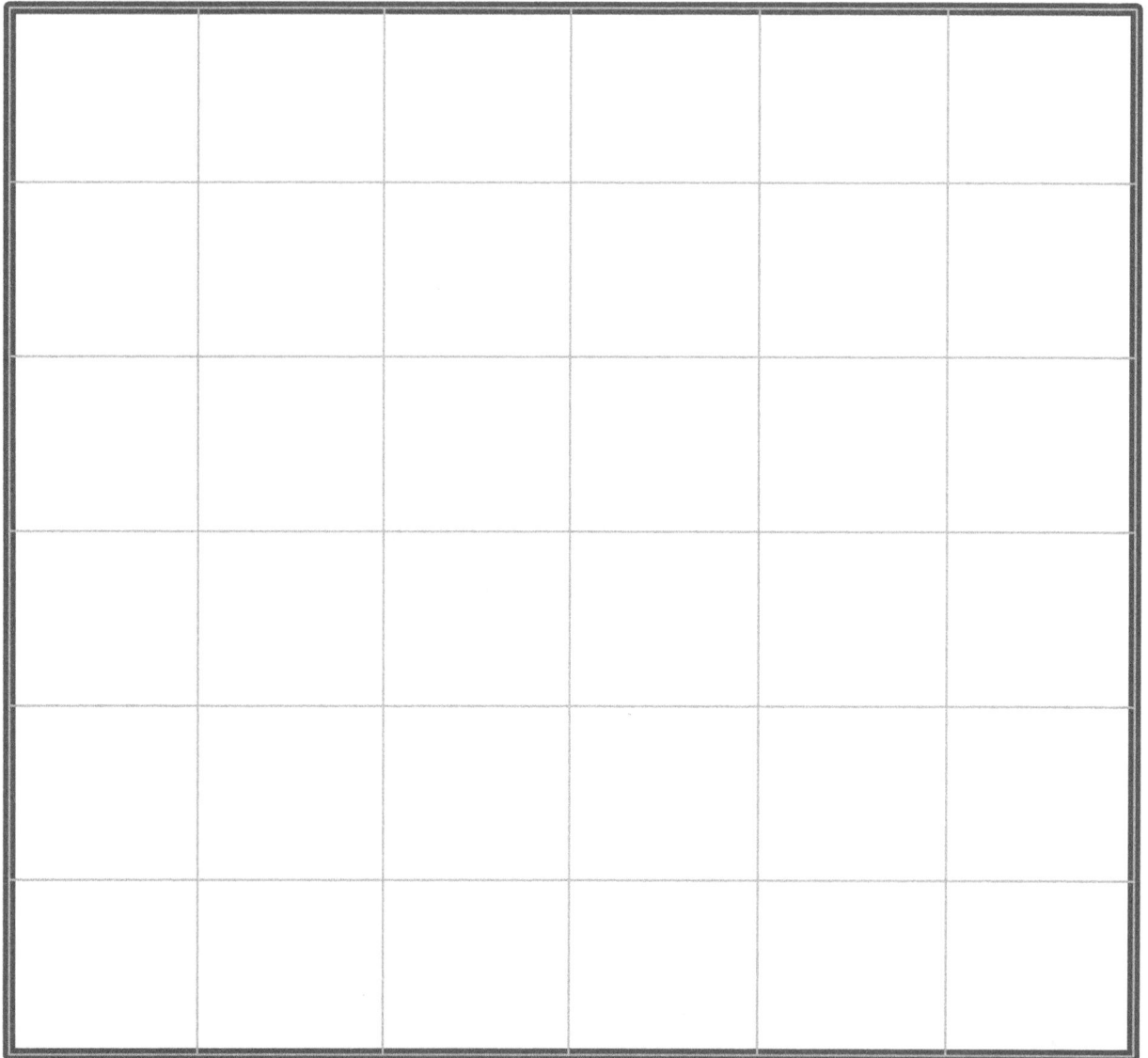

DRAW
THE
IMAGE

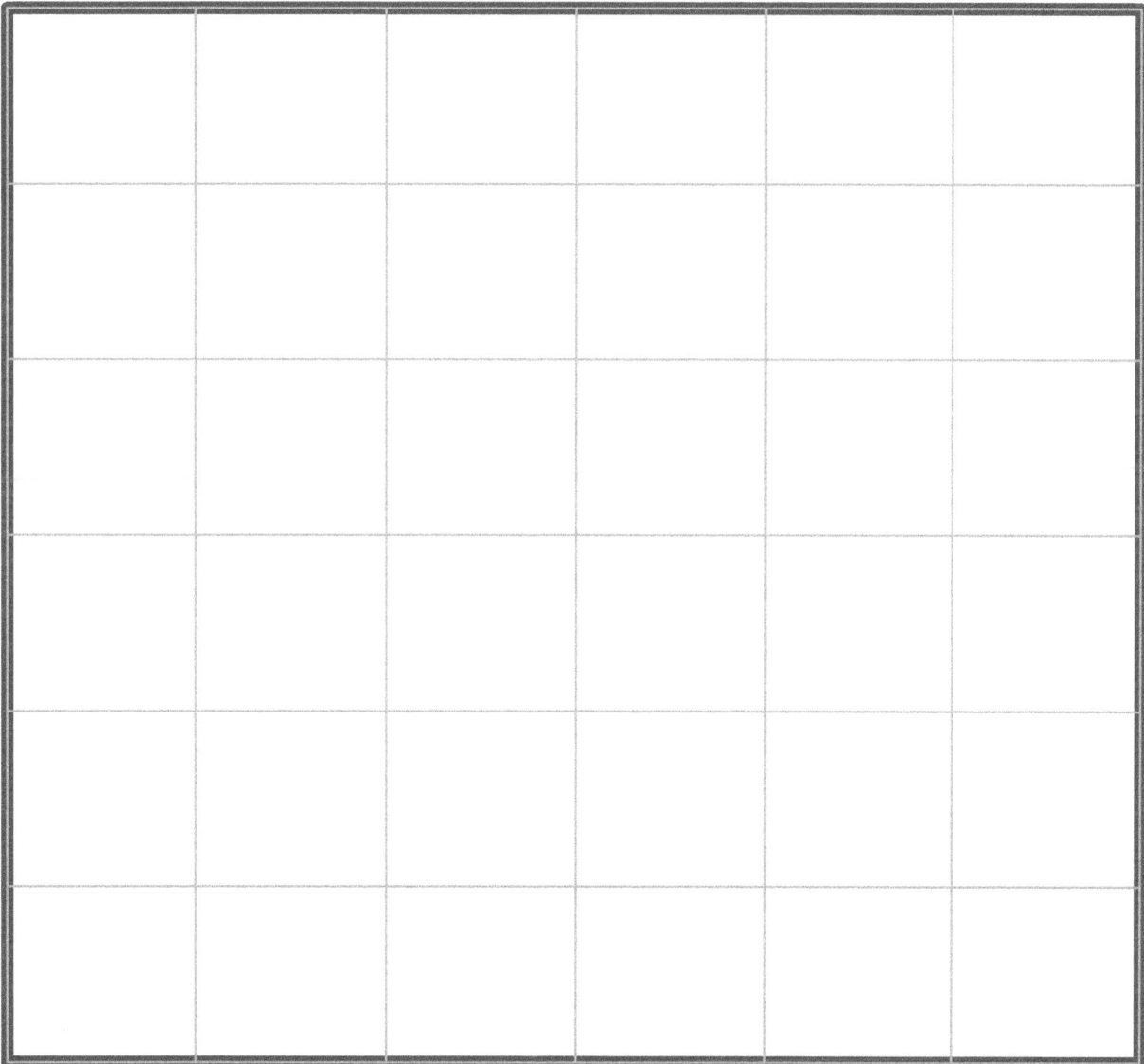

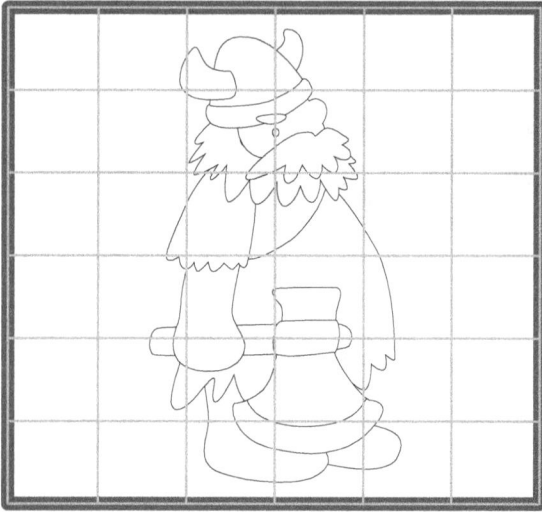

DRAW
THE
IMAGE

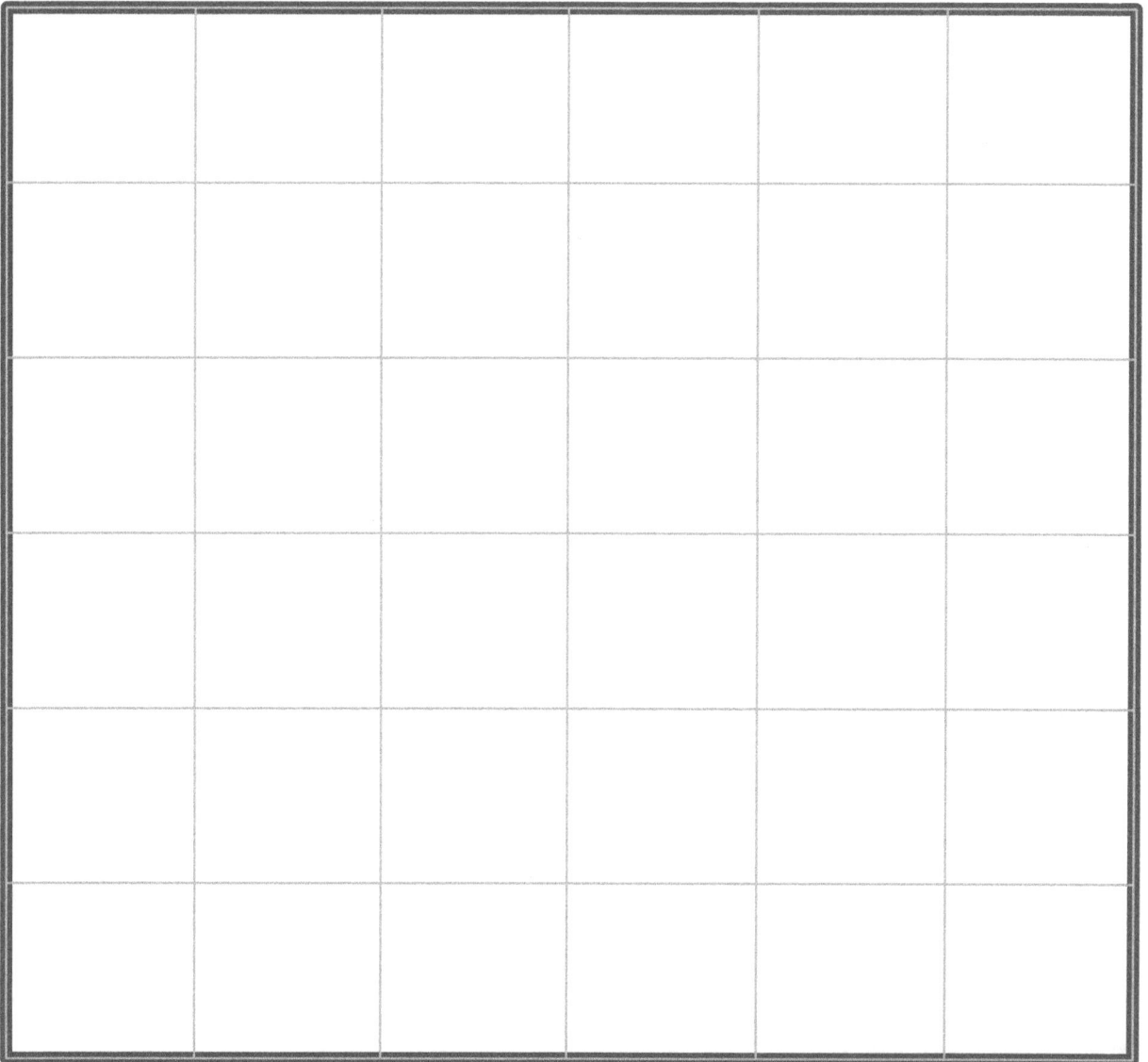

DRAW
THE
IMAGE

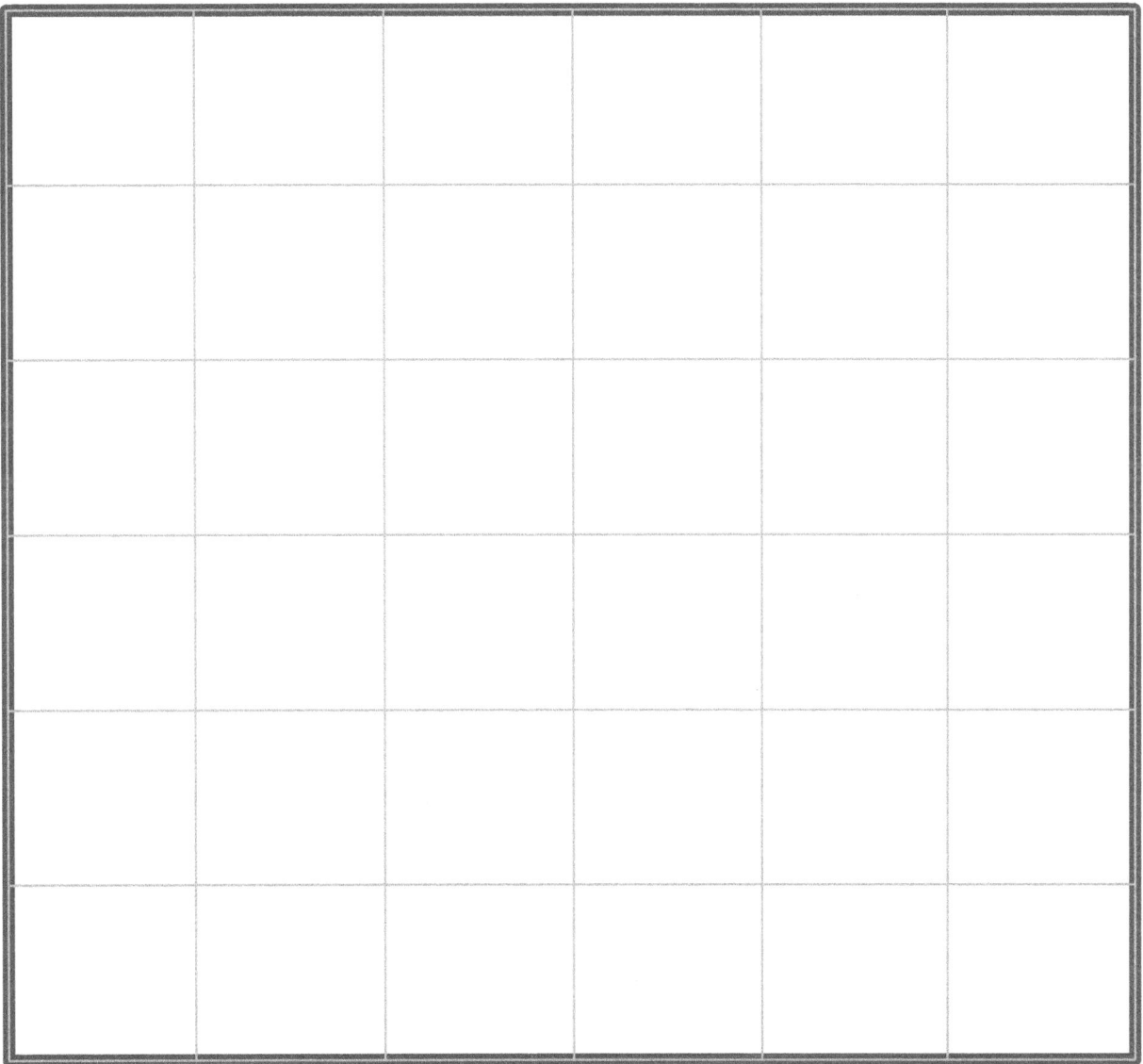

DRAW
THE
IMAGE

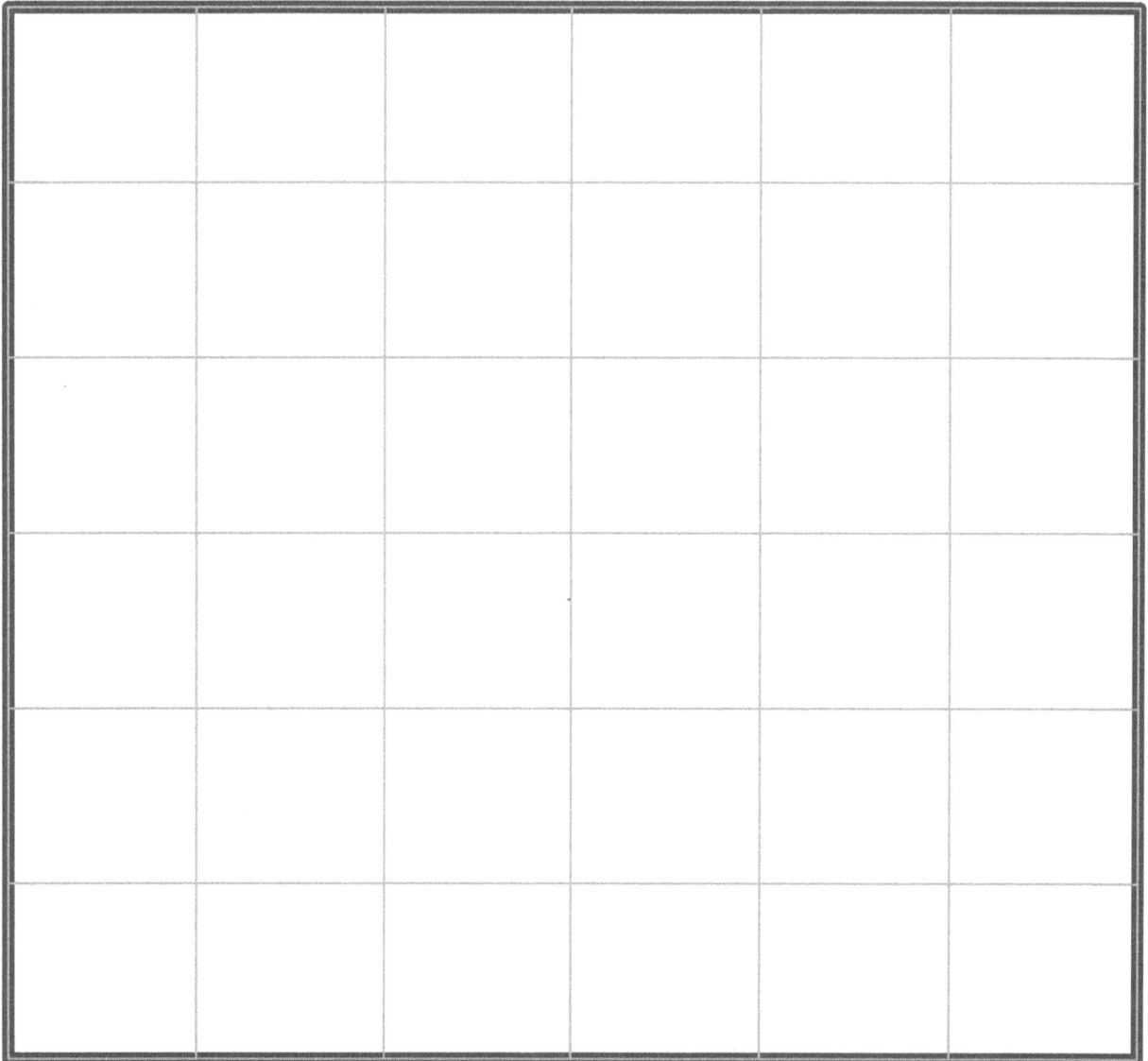

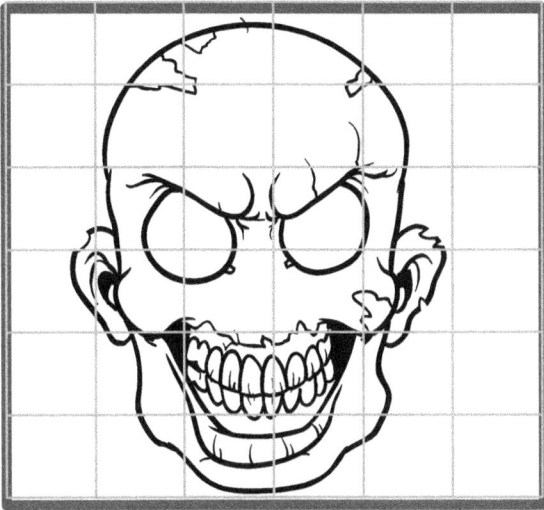

DRAW
THE
IMAGE

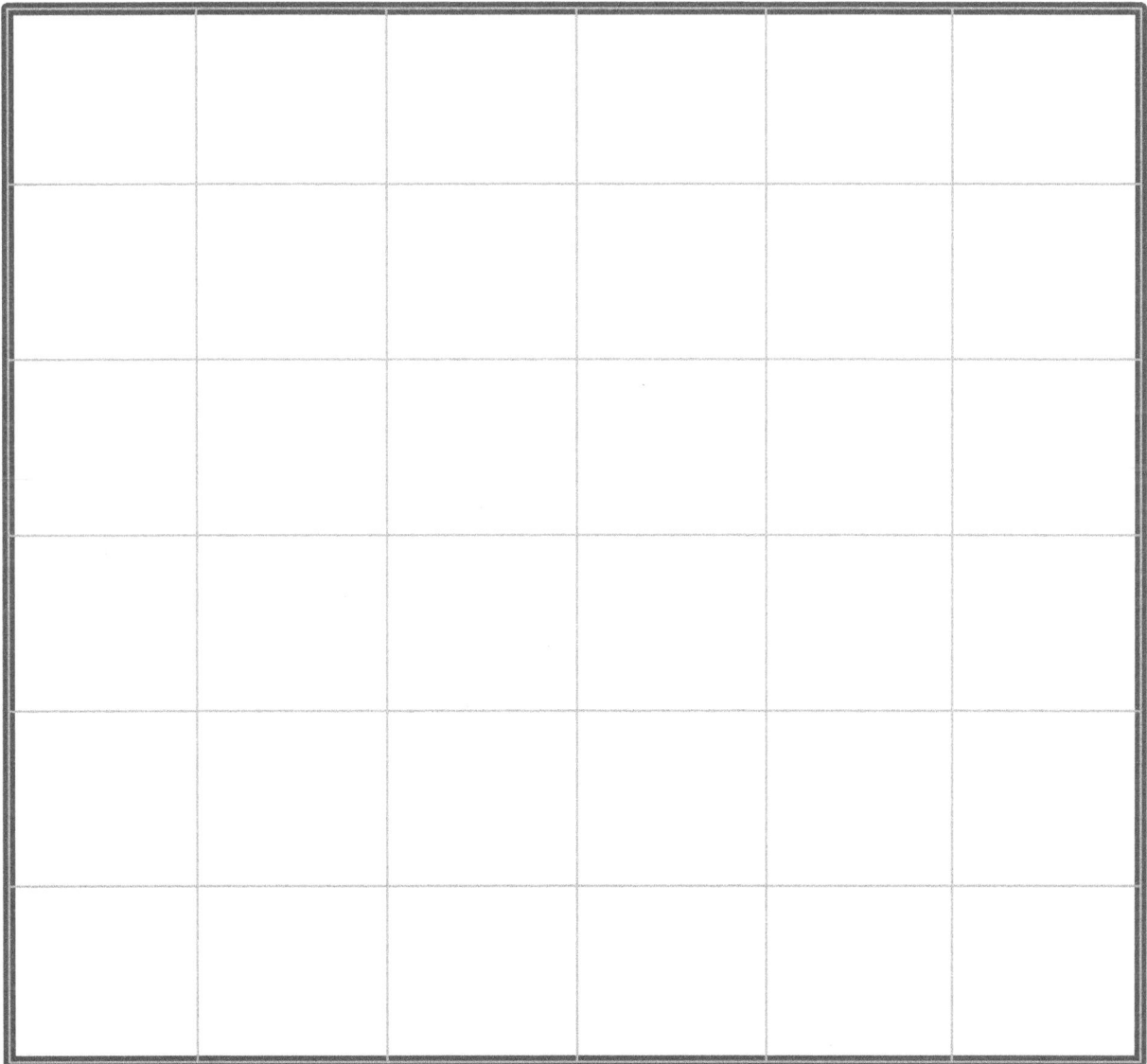

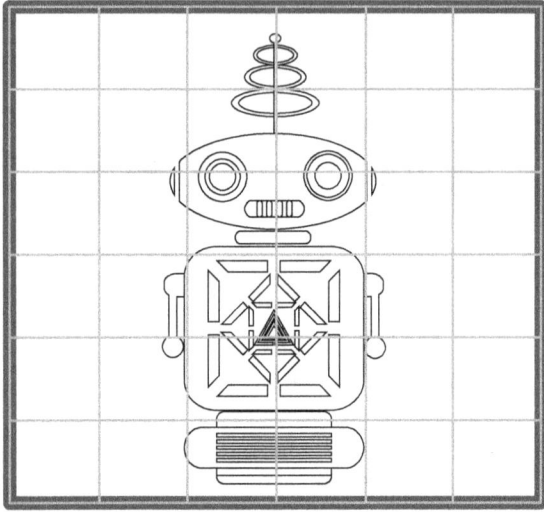

DRAW
THE
IMAGE

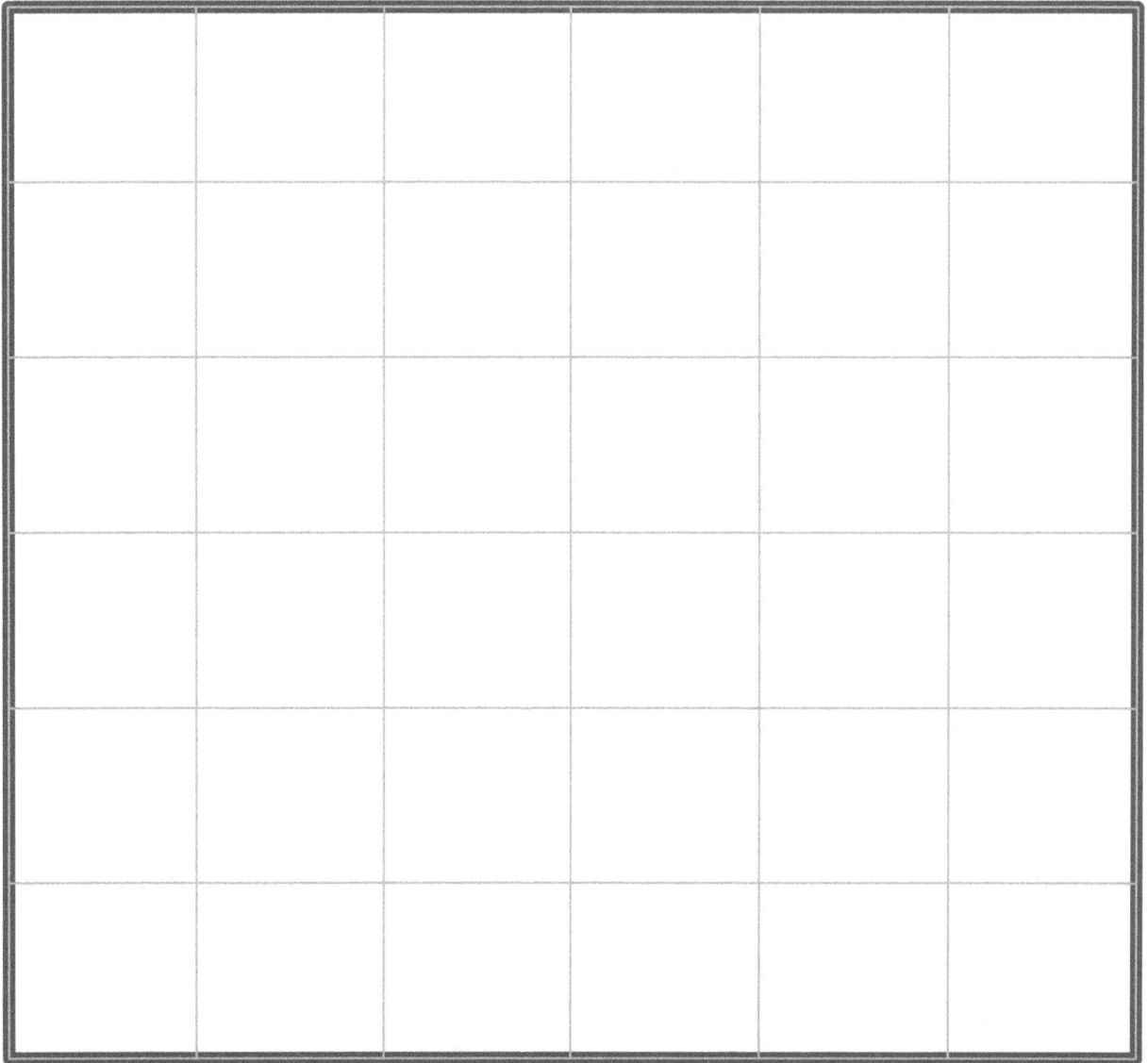

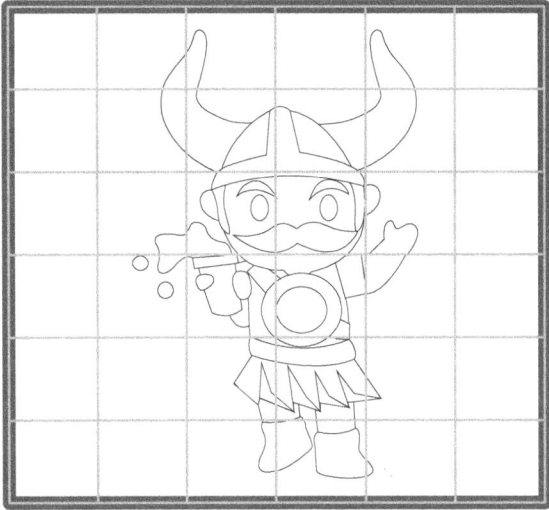

DRAW
THE
IMAGE

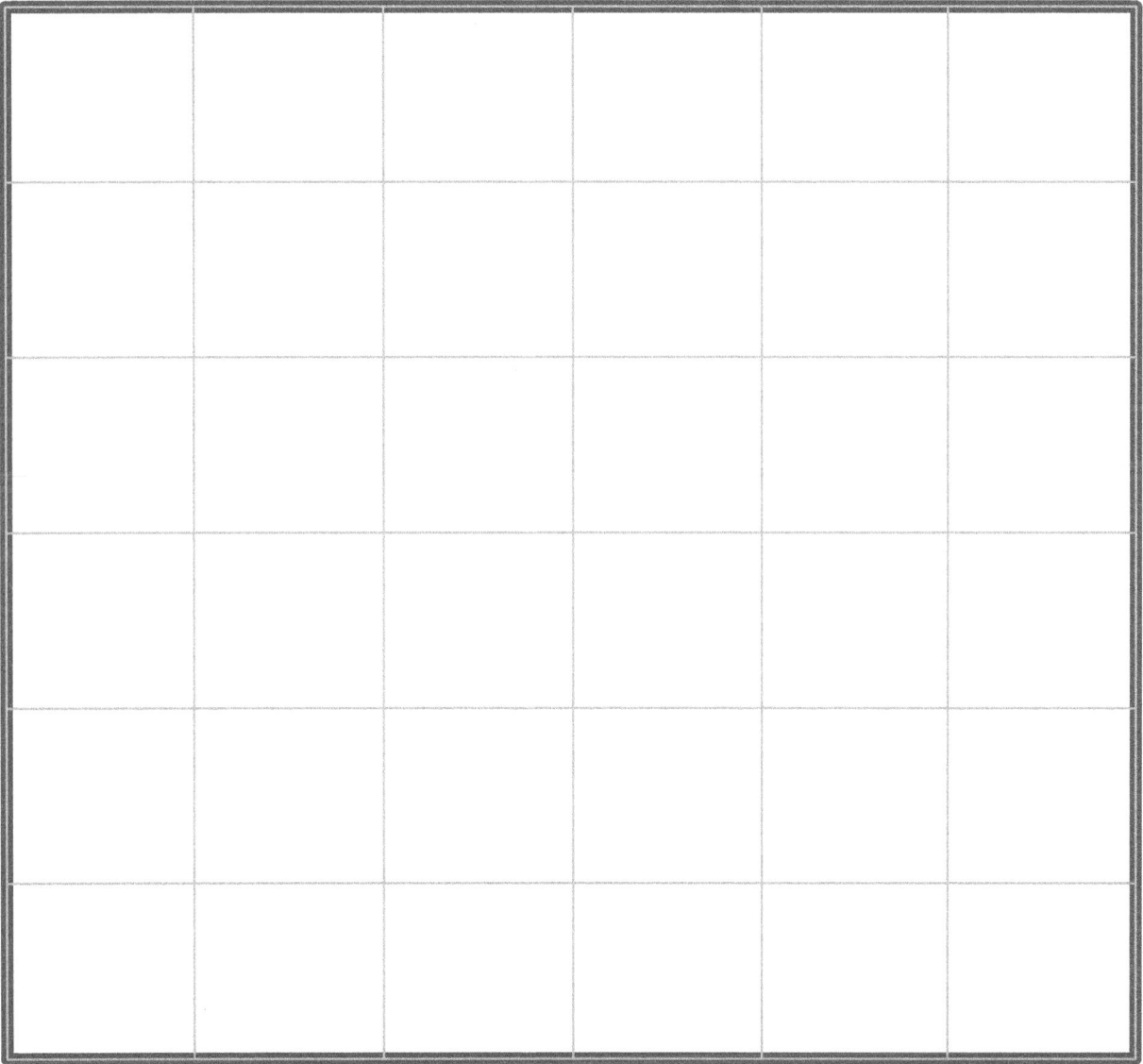

DRAW
THE
IMAGE

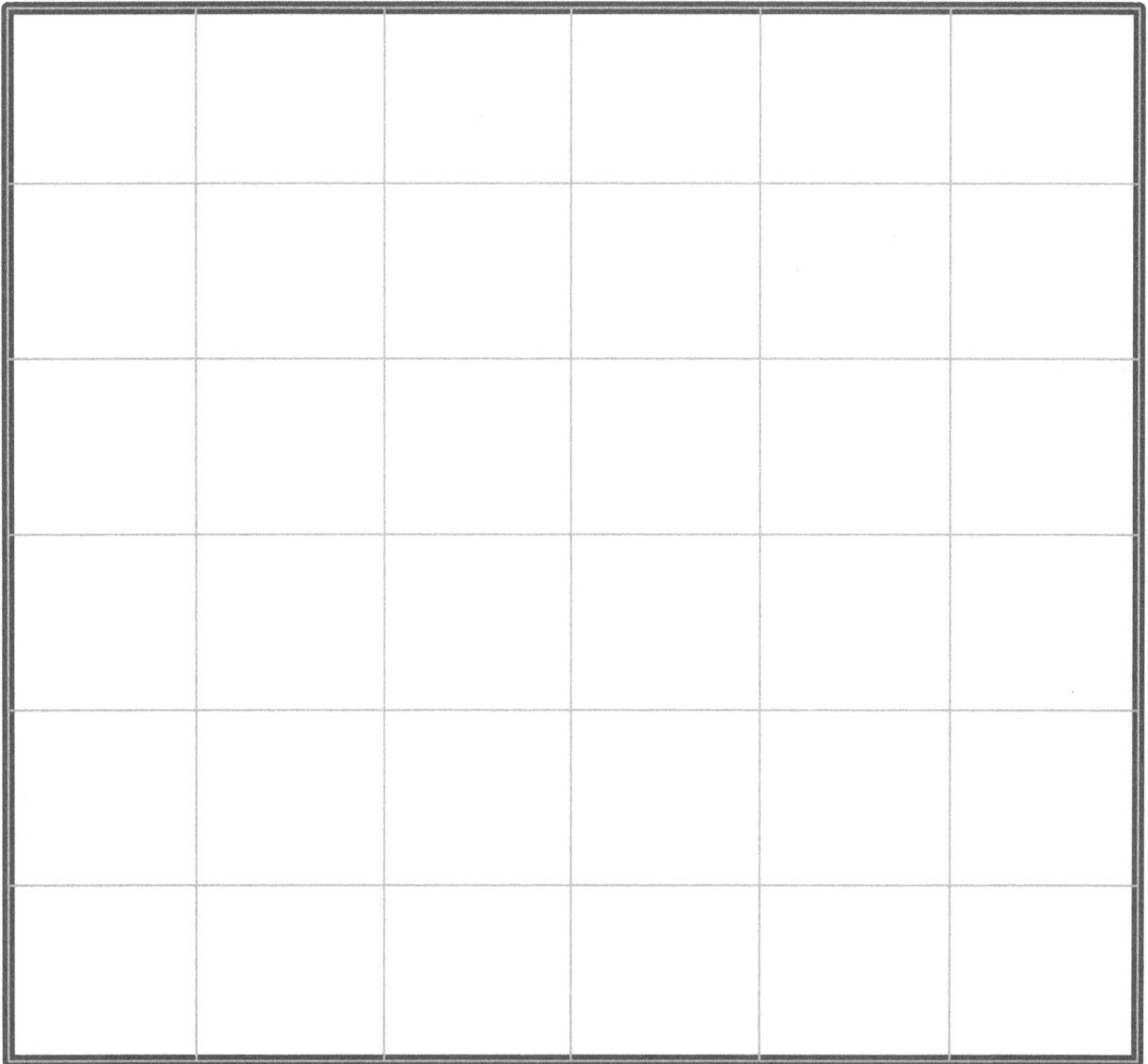

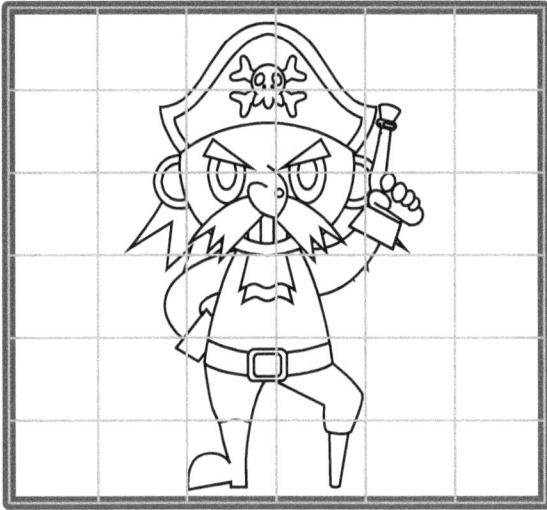

DRAW
THE
IMAGE

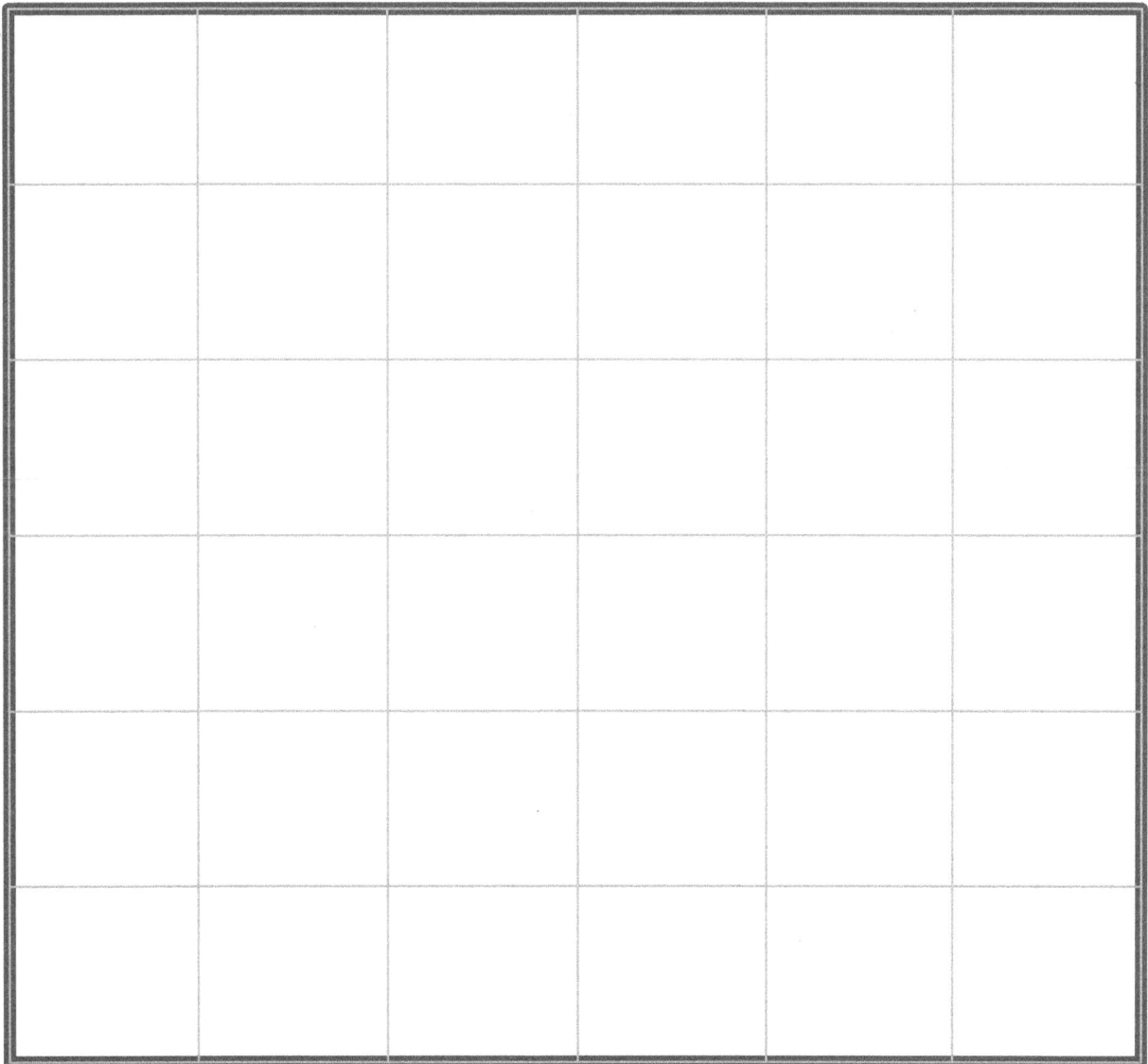

DRAW
THE
IMAGE

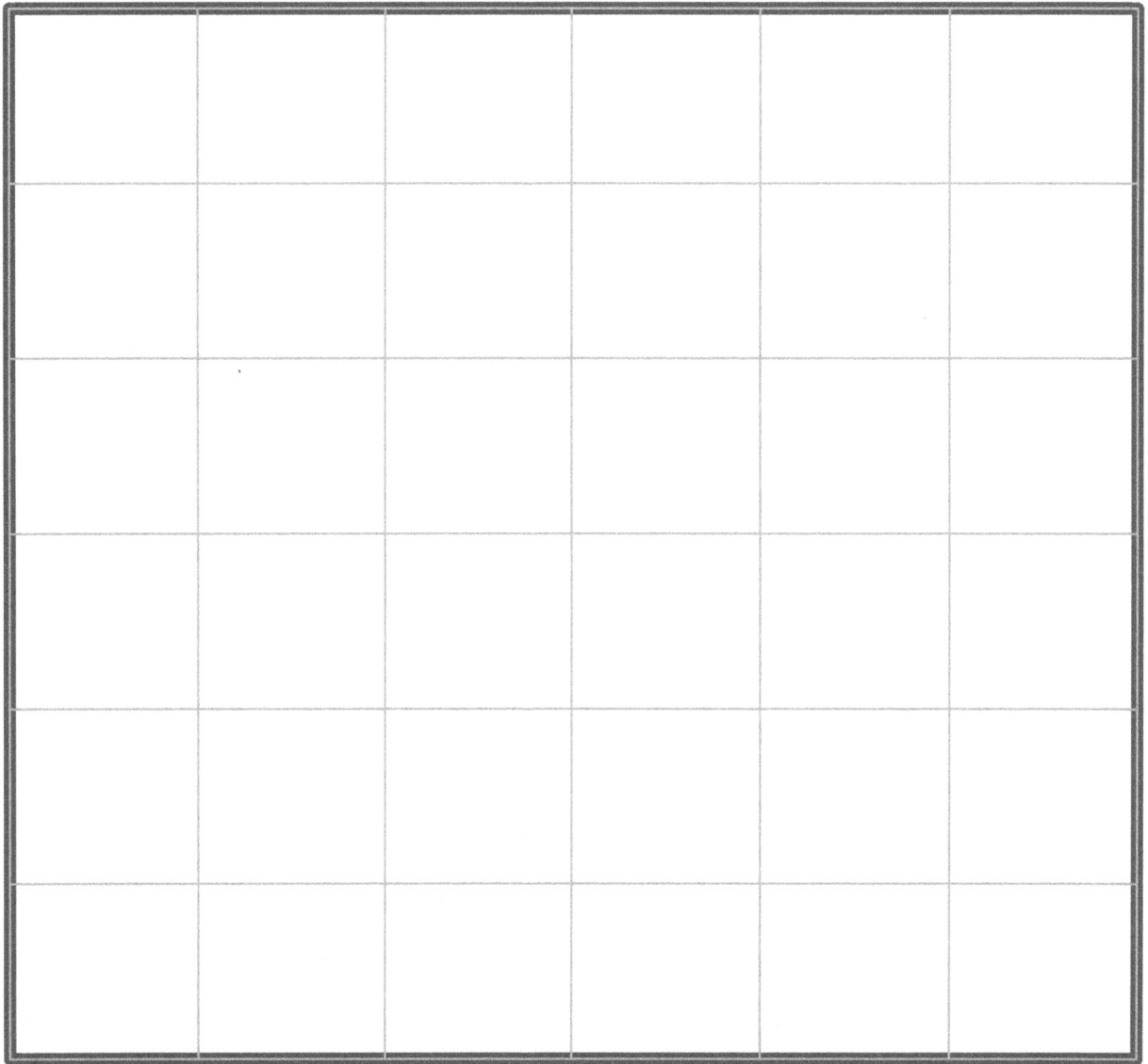

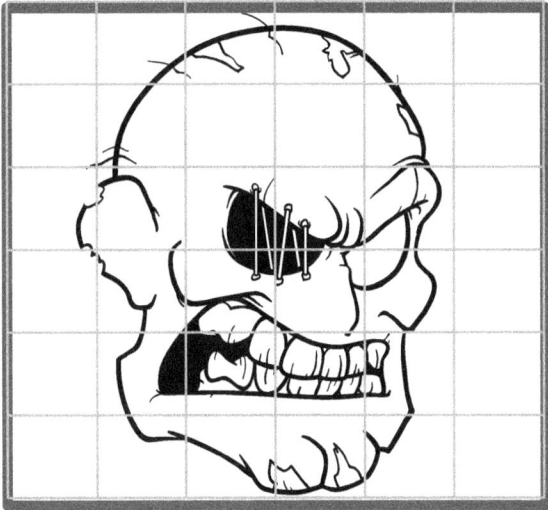

DRAW
THE
IMAGE

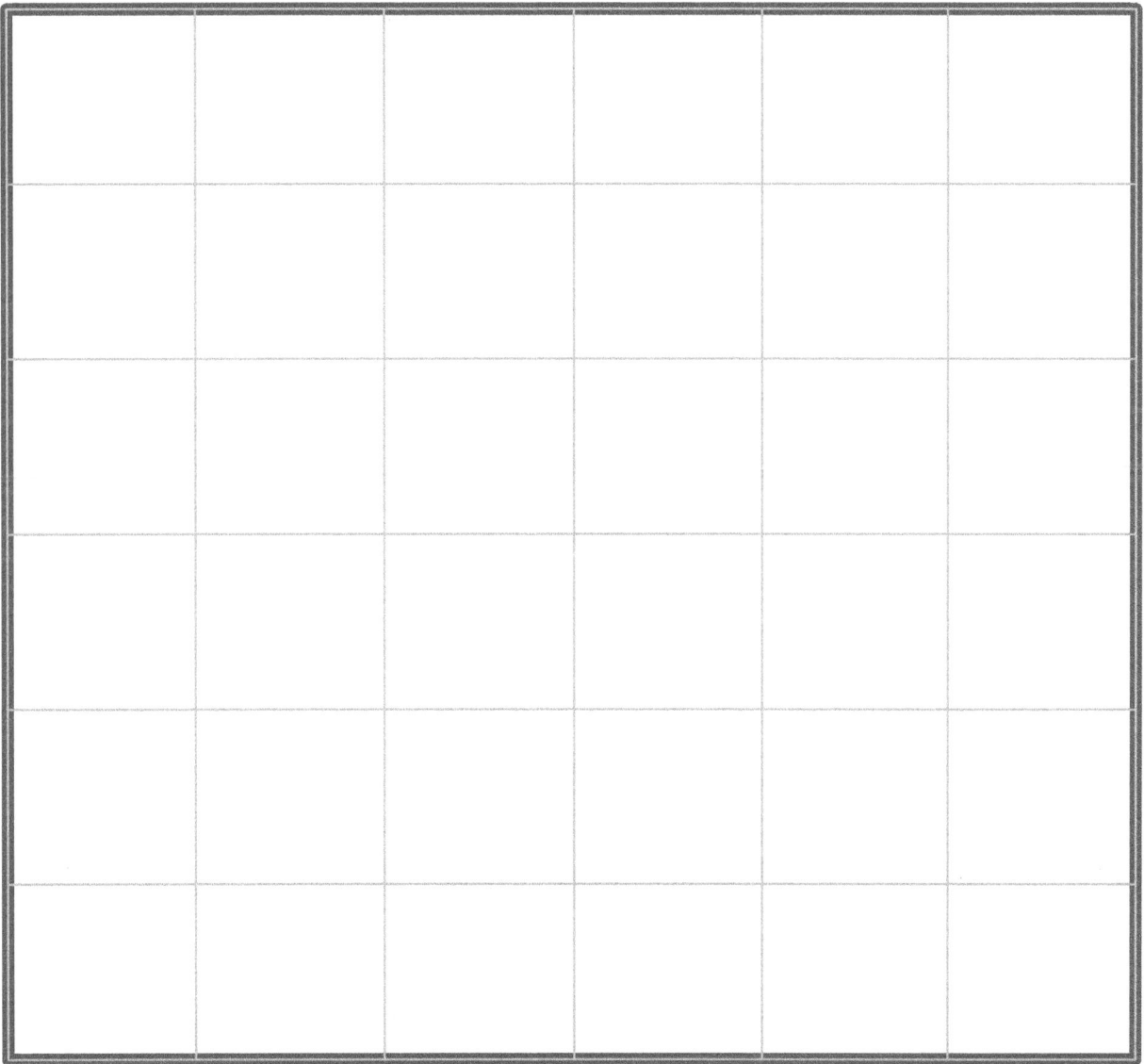

DRAW
THE
IMAGE

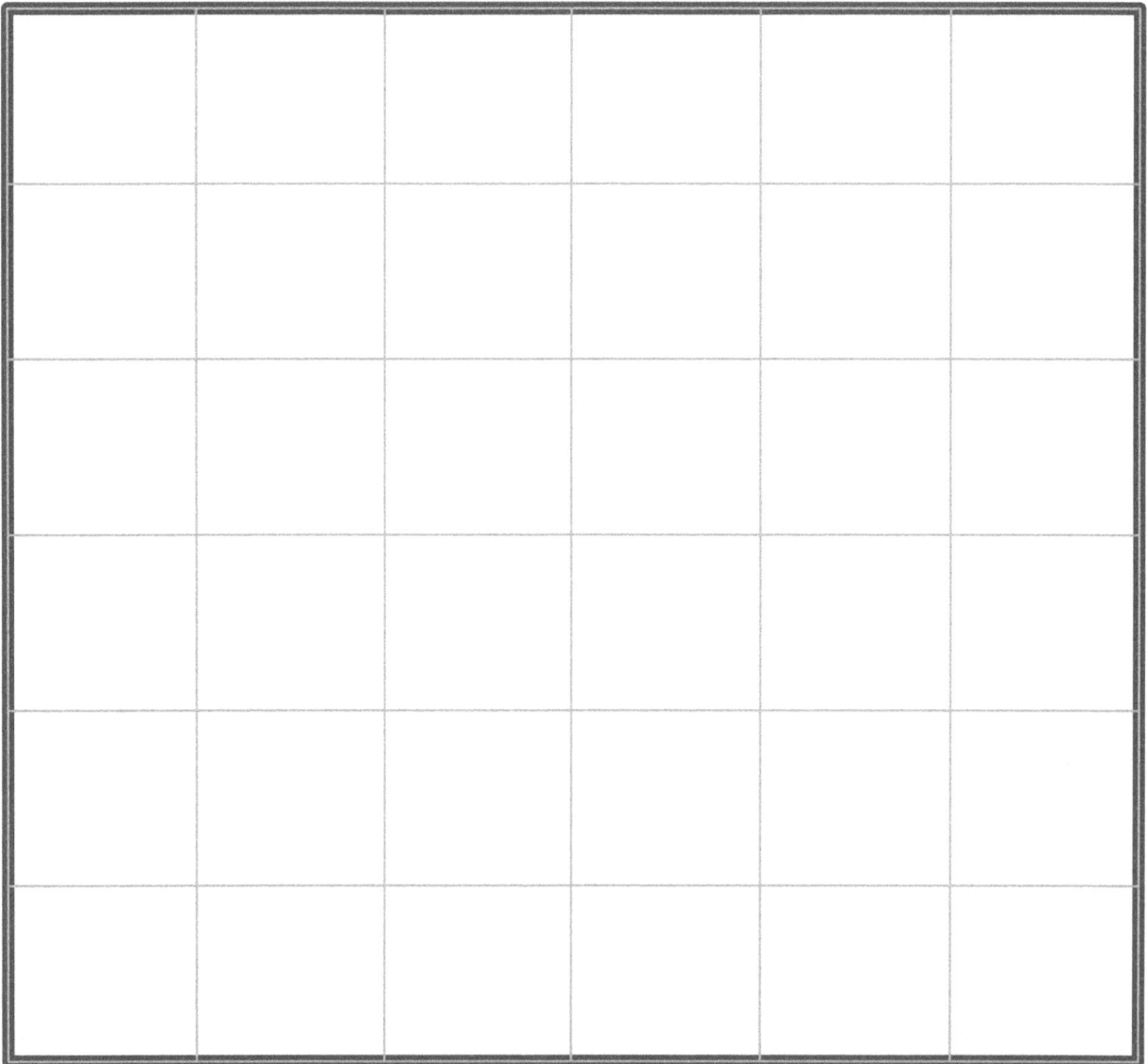

DRAW
THE
IMAGE

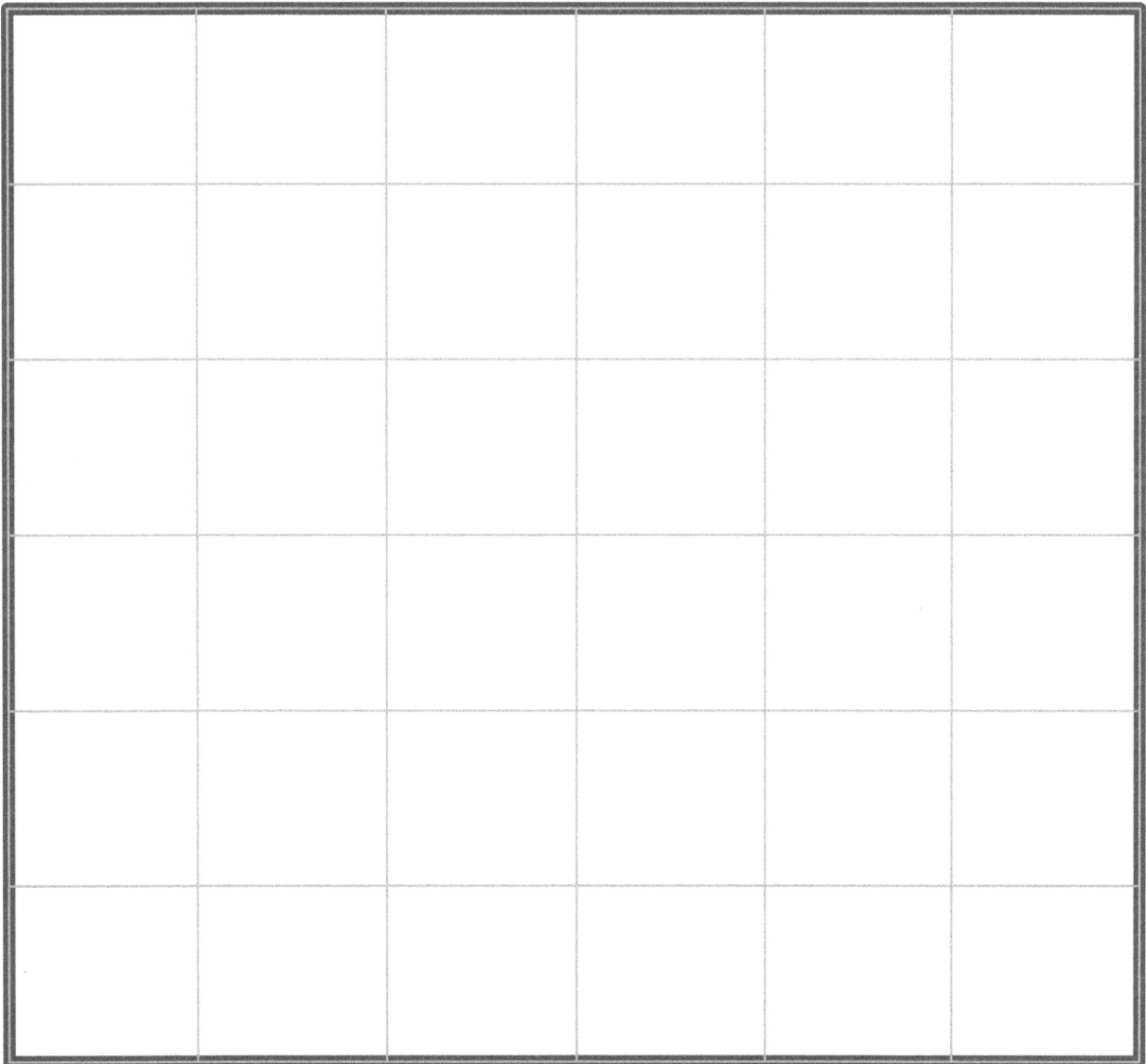

DRAW
THE
IMAGE

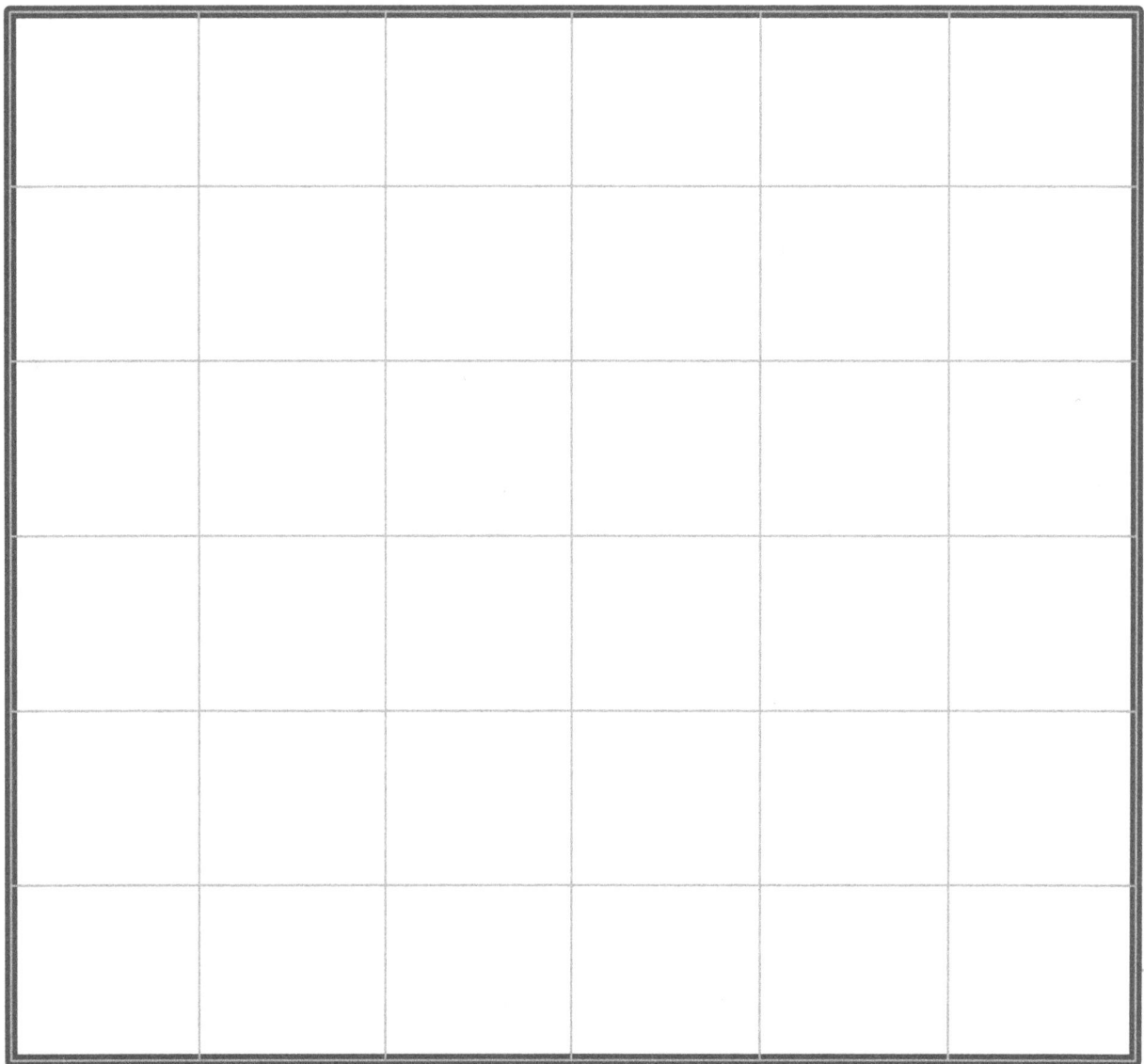

DRAW
THE
IMAGE

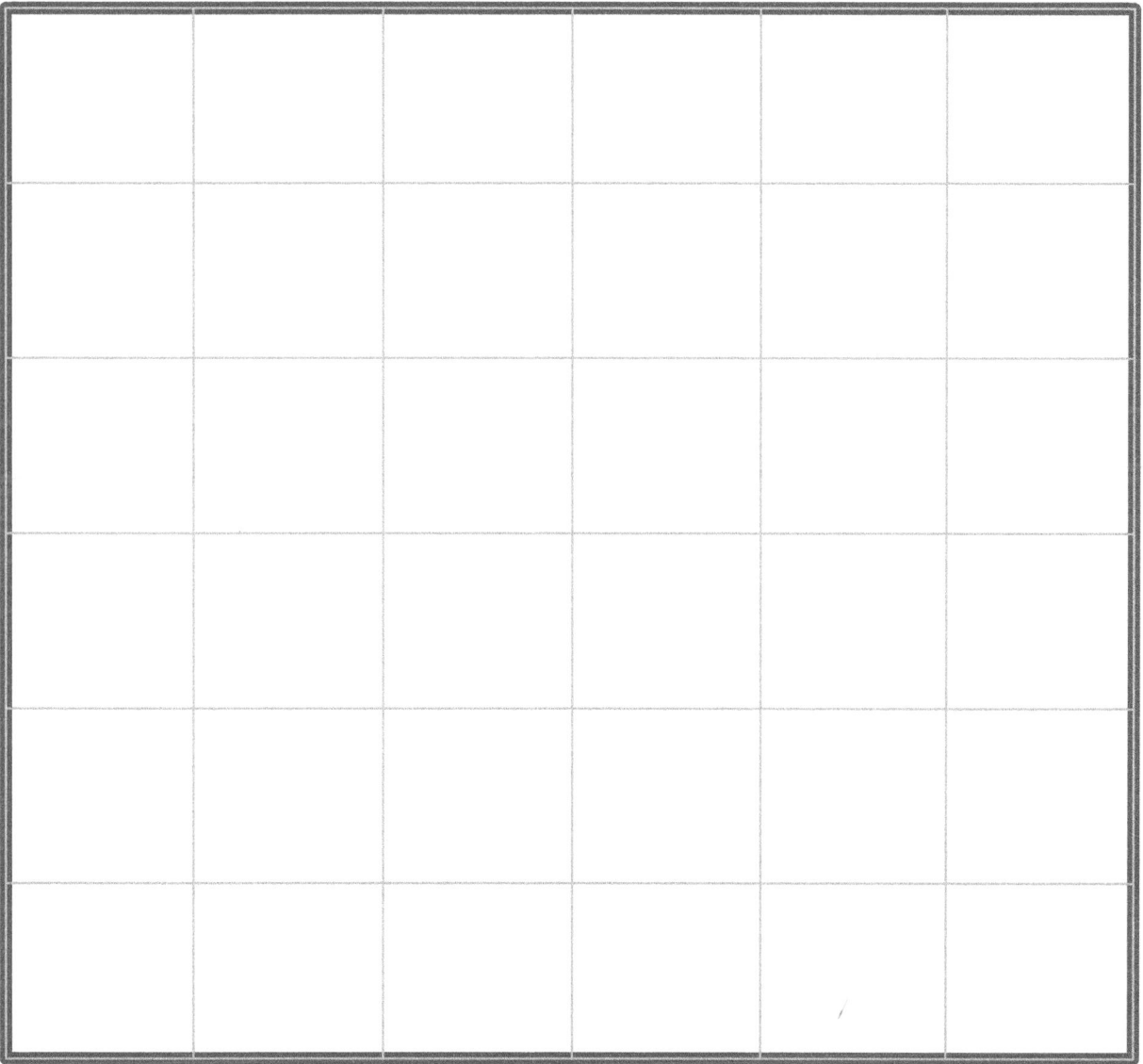

www.ingramcontent.com/pod-product-compliance
Lightning Source LLC
LaVergne TN
LVHW082323080426
835508LV00042B/1517

ISBN 978-1-68321-412-0

9 781683 214120

90000

Pursuing PERFECT HAND DRAWN ANIMALS

a How to Activity Book

ACTIVIBOOKS FOR KIDS